The Employment Portfolio

IDENTIFYING SKILLS, TRAINING, ACCOMPLISHMENTS, AND REFERENCES FOR THE JOB SEEKER

Charles P. Bostaph, Ph.D.

Roland B. Vendeland, M.Ed.

Prentice Hall

Upper Saddle River, New Jersey 07458

Library of Congress Cataloging-in-Publication Data

Bostaph, Charles.
    The employment portfolio : identifying skills, training,
accomplishments, and references for the job seeker / Charles
Bostaph, Roland B. Vendeland.
      p.   cm.
   Includes index.
   ISBN 0–13–956699–6
   1. Employment portfolios.   I. Vendeland, Roland B.
HF5383.B567   2000
650.14—DC21   99–19736
                                                       CIP
                                                       Rev.

Publisher: *Carol Carter*
Acquisitions Editor: *Sande Johnson*
Managing Editor: *Mary Carnis*
In-House Liaison: *Glenn Johnston*
Production: *Holcomb Hathaway, Inc.*
Director of Manufacturing and Production: *Bruce Johnson*
Manufacturing Buyer: *Marc Bove*
Editorial Assistant: *Michelle M. Williams*
Marketing Manager: *Jeff McIlroy*
Marketing Assistant: *Barbara Rosenberg*

Copyright © 2000 by Prentice-Hall, Inc.
Upper Saddle River, New Jersey 07458

Printed in the United States of America

10 9 8 7 6 5 4 3 2

ISBN 0-13-956699-6

Prentice-Hall International (UK) Limited, *London*
Prentice-Hall of Australia Pty. Limited, *Sydney*
Prentice-Hall Canada Inc., *Toronto*
Prentice-Hall Hispanoamericana, S.A., *Mexico*
Prentice-Hall of India Private Limited, *New Delhi*
Prentice-Hall of Japan, Inc., *Tokyo*
Pearson Education Asia Pte. Ltd., *Singapore*
Editora Prentice-Hall do Brasil, Ltda., *Rio de Janeiro*
Prentice-Hall, Upper Saddle River, *New Jersey*

CONTENTS

**CHAPTER 4: 58 EXAMPLES OF TABLES OF CONTENTS
FOR YOUR S.T.A.R. PORTFOLIO   49**

FOREWORD

This book can make a real difference in your life!

Your two authors have devoted their lives to helping people find not just a job, but a great job! How have they accomplished this? Both have succeeded by developing and applying the newest and best ideas to the career search.

They now show you how to use one of their most powerful job search tools: the S.T.A.R. Portfolio. With the use of this system, not only will you be able to *describe* your accomplishments, but you will also be able to *demonstrate* to each potential employer what you have actually achieved. Students praise the S.T.A.R. System, claiming that it has given them an extra "edge" in securing their special job.

Finding a job is a challenge, perhaps one of the most important challenges in your life. The S.T.A.R. Portfolio System can be an invaluable tool in meeting this challenge.

Wishing you great success in your career search!

Linda Parrish Sullivan
Professor of Hospitality Management
Community College of Allegheny County

PREFACE

You have probably heard about "portfolios" from your teachers, colleagues, or friends. You wonder, "What is a portfolio and why do I need one?" You know that artists have been using portfolios for centuries to demonstrate their talents and abilities to employers, buyers, and patrons. But even though you are probably not an artist in the literal sense of the word, you begin to realize the enormous advantages of showing someone the results of your labors and skills. With your portfolio displayed in front of you, you can talk about the results of your work with enthusiasm and pride. Now you are beginning to form a picture, although sketchy, of how you might use a portfolio for your job search or for advancing your career. In fact, let us, the authors, help guide you through the process of developing an employment vehicle called the S.T.A.R. Portfolio, which represents Skills, Training, Accomplishments, and References. S.T.A.R. can help you get job interviews and ultimately the job you want.

WHY YOU MIGHT NEED A PORTFOLIO!

First of all, you might need a portfolio to help you gain some confidence in yourself. After you have listed all the things you have done and documented them through actual samples, photos, letters, papers, awards, skills, and so on, you will be surprised how impressive your work and accomplishments are thus far in your life. You will also be able to see that your accomplishments are pointing you in the right career direction or career path. Maybe your portfolio needs some more pieces to fit into the larger puzzle before the picture starts to become clearly focused. Visualize the results of your portfolio through the many experiences you already have. The process of creating your portfolio is ongoing. Your portfolio will continue to grow and change with you as your career develops. It can help show you the way to the next step along your career path, and it can give you confidence in your good work. You can use it over and over again when you are searching for a job, changing careers, looking for a promotion, being evaluated, or asking for a raise. We think that we are giving you more than just good advice in developing and maintaining your portfolio. An employment portfolio as organized and professional as the S.T.A.R. Portfolio may be the career builder that you need. The S.T.A.R. Portfolio will help you gain a foothold on your future in order to gain greater employment opportunities and promotions.

HOW CAN THE S.T.A.R. PORTFOLIO HELP ME GET A JOB?

The S.T.A.R. Portfolio can help you in three ways. One, it can help you prepare for an employment interviewer's questions and help you develop your answers once you are prepared to discuss tangible Skills, Training, Accomplishments, and References. You can answer almost any of the interviewer's questions with your S.T.A.R. Portfolio. Second, you will have documentation to impress the employer and interviewer. The interviewer may keep this documentation to remind him or her of you and your interview. The employment interviewer may even share your documentation with his or her colleagues, supervisor, and associates on your behalf. Third, you can use the S.T.A.R. Portfolio to help you secure a job interview through a telephone conversation or to enhance your resume, as mentioned in Chapter Three. This approach is obvious and sensible, but also one that requires you to do some extensive preparation in compiling your portfolio. The better your portfolio is, the better it will work for you.

GET STARTED!

The S.T.A.R. Portfolio can be fun to prepare. You will be able to make contacts with many people who are currently working in a career field that interests you as you gather materials for your portfolio. You might renew former job contacts as a result of asking them for their advice and assistance. Get started now and use your portfolio to get a career and a job that you will truly like and enjoy. The S.T.A.R. Portfolio can help you shape a bright future.

ACKNOWLEDGMENTS

This book is the product of a collaboration effort from an idea that Roland originally developed from his work with students, especially returning students whom he thought might benefit from reflecting upon, reviewing, and documenting their previous background and skills. We wish to acknowledge these students, who have motivated us to write this book. Appreciation also goes out to a long list of people who have been supportive in our effort with advice for creating and implementing the S.T.A.R. Portfolio. Many thanks go out to Professor Linda Sullivan, who has given us support, energy for renewal, and insights from her classroom portfolios. A special thanks and acknowledgment to Donna Cipriani, Frank Catanzaro, and Keith Eustace for allowing us to use their portfolios for actual demonstrations in our book and to John Mirenzi for allowing us to use samples of his artwork in Chapter 5. We would be remiss if we did not recognize our excellent editorial staff at Prentice Hall, including Michelle Williams, Sue Bierman, and Ray Mesing; our readers, Elaine Ader, Montgomery College (TX), Laurie Collins, Mission College (CA), Joe Ritchie, Indiana University of Pennsylvania, and Pat Schutz, Mesa State College (CO); our energetic typist, Michelle Gravante, and our assistant for initial typing and layout design, Patricia Catanzaro. As we mentioned, this book is an effort of many professional people in the college and community that we wish to thank and hope that they continue to share their expertise and encouragement with all of us. As a result of this effort, we hope our first edition will allow you to build a portfolio that you can use with confidence and enthusiasm to enrich your career and your life.

Charles P. Bostaph, Ph.D.
Roland B. Vendeland, M.Ed.

The Employment Portfolio

IDENTIFYING SKILLS, TRAINING, ACCOMPLISHMENTS, AND REFERENCES FOR THE JOB SEEKER

Five Types of Portfolios for Career Success

1

Portfolios are vehicles by which individuals systematically display empirical evidence of their skills, training, achievements, and references. Educators and career services professionals use portfolios for reasons ranging from improving instruction, career exploration, and testing competencies to increasing one's employability. Five types of portfolios used in educational and business settings are identified below for the career development professional.

■ **FIVE TYPES OF PORTFOLIOS**

1. Studio Arts/Design Portfolio
2. Professional Development Portfolio
3. Instructional/Assessment Portfolio
4. Career Guidance Portfolio
5. Employment Portfolio

You might be most interested in starting your S.T.A.R. Employment Portfolio immediately for your own career advancement. If so, skip this section and proceed to Chapter 2. S.T.A.R. is a designation or an acronym for those items you need to include in your portfolio: Skills, Training, Accomplishments, and References.

1. STUDIO ARTS/DESIGN PORTFOLIO

You might recall Titian as an innovative Northern Renaissance artist who brought life to his paintings through realistic but flattering portrayals of his subjects with rich, lavish use of basic colors. You may not, however, credit him with the marketing and promotion of his portrait of Emperor Charles V to ensure his successful career as Italy's most prominent portrait painter. With his sketches of the emperor in hand or at least under his arm, Titian visited Pope Paul III and proposed to paint the Pope's portrait. The Charles V painting spoke for itself. The Pope was impressed with the richness of the painting and with Titian's talent. Not willing to have secular personages illuminated in grander fashion than himself, the Pope commissioned Titian to paint his portrait. Titian had utilized his portfolio to gain his most important consignment. He became the official papal artist through the successful demonstration of his studio arts portfolio.

Artists, designers, architects, photographers, and others use the studio arts/design portfolio to display samples of their work to contract with employers for more projects. This studio arts/design portfolio offers a history of their best work and commissions.

INFORMATION AGE

As the information age continues to explode, you will increasingly discover these portfolios presented electronically, featuring scanned photographs of artwork, projects created through computer-assisted design (CAD), digitally produced and developed photography, and immediate transmission of samples through downloading and e-mail. The studio arts/design portfolio, the oldest known form, can employ the most modern of technical applications. Some current examples of these are utilized at Carnegie-Mellon University in Pittsburgh and the University of Miami in Florida.

CARNEGIE-MELLON UNIVERSITY

Carnegie-Mellon University's Department of Architecture publishes the annual student publication, *Portfolio,* on-line. Previously published on paper, *Portfolio* presents a broad collection of students' work that is judged by the student editorial staff. The on-line publication, found at http://www.arc.cmu.edu, provides students with an electronic venue to showcase their work.

UNIVERSITY OF MIAMI

The University of Miami School of Architecture has established on-line presentations of students' architectural portfolios. The students design and document their work on computers and display it on the Web at http://www.arc.miami.edu. Architecture faculty members from around the world review and critique the presentations via e-mail. This opens up foreign as well as domestic employment opportunities for students upon completion of their studies.

Architecture students also create their own Web sites. Maintaining them is time-consuming, but creating and maintaining Web sites gives students the opportunity to demonstrate their digital technology and design skills. In the future, sound and video will be incorporated into these presentations, which will add acoustics and movement to still images. The impact is equivalent to that of television advertising in contrast to magazine print.

2. PROFESSIONAL DEVELOPMENT PORTFOLIO

Teaching professionals use the professional development portfolio to assess and improve their own instruction. The professional development portfolio is also called a "teaching dossier" or a "teaching portfolio." During their pre-service training and continuing into their careers, teachers develop portfolios of materials and techniques with which they can critically examine and improve the effectiveness of their instruction in a demonstrative format.

Seldin (1997), through a review of 400 samples, identifies these most frequent inclusions in teaching portfolios:

■ TEACHING PORTFOLIOS: MATERIALS FROM ONESELF

- descriptions of teaching responsibilities and techniques
- course syllabi
- descriptions of personal development
- instructional innovations

- statement of teaching goals

■ TEACHING PORTFOLIOS: MATERIALS FROM OTHERS

- student evaluations
- colleague observations
- documentation of teaching development activity
- colleague review of teaching materials
- recognition received

In the United States, colleges and universities are increasingly using professional development portfolios to evaluate the teaching effectiveness of their faculty members for contract renewal and granting tenure, awarding merit pay, and providing recognition. Seldin (1997) reports approximately 75 institutions using or developing teaching portfolios in 1991, 400 in 1993, and over 1,000 in 1997. Contents vary, but most often the portfolios include the box to the right.

In its most popular application, the professional development portfolio permits teaching professionals to improve their instructional skills and to be held accountable for their performance.

> ### PROFESSIONAL DEVELOPMENT PORTFOLIO
>
> 1. Planning and preparation materials
> 2. Classroom instruction materials
> 3. Evaluation materials
> 4. Professional development materials

3. INSTRUCTIONAL/ASSESSMENT PORTFOLIO

An ever-increasing number of educators have implemented portfolio development as a means of student instruction and student performance assessment to adapt to the national trend toward performance-based education and authentic assessment.

The instructional/assessment portfolio is a tool used to select, evaluate, document, and prescribe students' work. It serves as a longitudinal exhibit of students' growth and performance. With teacher assistance, students can create, choose, and justify their selections for portfolio inclusion. Teachers evaluate students based on students' assembled portfolios. Teachers can then revise their instruction to meet the needs of the students as revealed by the portfolios.

Despite wide variations in the applications and inclusions of instructional/assessment portfolios, a general consensus exists regarding their purpose and content.

■ PURPOSE OF INSTRUCTIONAL/ASSESSMENT PORTFOLIO

- alignment of instruction, assessment, and curriculum
- student acquisition of self-knowledge, problem-solving skills, higher-order thinking skills, and responsibility for own learning
- longitudinal tracking of students' achievement, and progress
- purposeful collection of student work
- emphasis on process and product
- holistic, student-centered approach
- performance-based, project-oriented authentic assessment
- application of learning to everyday life
- demonstration of competence
- student self-assessment and reflection

■ CONTENT OF INSTRUCTIONAL/ASSESSMENT PORTFOLIO

- student-created and -selected work samples
- student rationale for selection of samples
- student description of included samples

- self-assessments
- self-reflections

In summary, instructional/assessment portfolios support instruction, align instruction with curriculum, and serve as authentic assessments of students' performance.

LIFE WORK PORTFOLIO

1. Who I am
2. Exploring
3. Deciding
4. Planning and acting

EDUCATION PORTFOLIO (GRADES 9–12)

1. *Student and school information* such as courses, grades, and activities
2. Identification of *career areas of interests* through research, volunteering, and employment
3. *Self-assessment information* including career tests and autobiographies
4. High school *course planning* in math, science, and languages in conjunction with career goals and options

CAREER PORTFOLIO

1. Introduction
2. Self-portrait
3. Education plan
4. Career plan
5. Conclusion

PROFESSIONAL NURSING PORTFOLIO

1. knowledge base for nursing practice
2. process of nursing care
3. evaluation of nursing competence and effectiveness
4. nursing philosophy
5. nursing skills
6. practice environment

4. CAREER GUIDANCE PORTFOLIO

In 1976 Congress established the National Occupation Information Coordinating Committee (NOICC) to deal with labor information and career development needs of youth and adults. An outgrowth of this initiative was the Career Development Portfolio project emphasizing self-knowledge, educational and occupational exploration, and career planning. The Career Development Training Institute (CDTI), under a grant from the National Occupational Information Coordinating Committee, developed the life work portfolio. The contents fall into four categories, as listed in the box to the left.

Career guidance portfolios cover a wider range of areas than career development portfolios. In fact, a variety of career development educational programs have evolved and are now using career guidance portfolios to demonstrate:

- career decision-making skills
- career awareness
- career readiness skills
- workplace skills/attitudes
- interview skills/attitudes
- exploration of career possibilities
- occupational skill clusters
- employment projections

Some of these portfolio contents for high school and college students can be reviewed in the next section. Note the differences between the high school and college portfolios.

OHIO CONSORTIUM FOR PORTFOLIO DEVELOPMENT

Wright State University, the University of Dayton, and Central State University formed the Ohio Consortium for Portfolio Development to develop goal setting and career decision making among high school students and adults. This career portfolio contained five sections, as shown in the box.

UNIVERSITY OF WISCONSIN—MADISON

The University of Wisconsin–Madison School of Nursing required its non-traditional nursing students to develop professional nursing portfolios. Faculty reviewed these portfolios, evaluated the relevance of students' non-college experience, placed students in appropriate course levels, and granted students educational credits. In addition to its use as a determinant for college credit and coursework, the nursing portfolio revealed accomplishments and experiences that led to choices and options for a nursing career. The completed nursing portfolio included professional, employment, and educational achievements.

In summary, the purpose of the career guidance portfolio is to provide students with insights into work-related skills and long-range career goals.

5. EMPLOYMENT PORTFOLIO

The required components of the employment portfolio serve as assessment vehicles that ensure comprehensiveness, which will likely impress prospective employers. The colleges below outline some of the significant points in creating the professional employment portfolio.

BRONX COMMUNITY COLLEGE

At the Bronx Community College in the Job Partners Training Act (JPTA) Adult Education Program, participants create employment portfolios to facilitate their job search through:

- learning how to practice presenting the portfolio during the interview
- showcasing trainee work readiness
- creating memorable impressions of skills, training, and enthusiasm
- focusing on assertive communication during the job interview

BALL STATE UNIVERSITY

Ball State's Career Services outlines the process of purpose, contents, and creation of a professional employment portfolio. The Service advises referencing the portfolio in both the resume and the cover letter. This information is featured on the Ball State University Career Services Web site, http://www.bus.edu/careers/foliojsb.html.

WITTENBERG UNIVERSITY

Wittenberg University assists its business administration and management students to "package evidence of their competencies for presentation at the interview." In addition to demonstrating competency, these portfolios serve as a professional tool to assist the job candidate in gaining control over and comfort in the interview, and thus reduce interview anxiety and nervousness.

Wittenberg students have incorporated eye-catching projects into their portfolios. These include demonstration videos, photos of trade show exhibits, and spreadsheet assignments. The University requested management alumni to describe a current typical first assignment and how best to demonstrate the competencies needed for such an assignment in a portfolio. Respondents suggested elements reflecting work style, such as group projects, employers' evaluations, professors' evaluations, project awards, team projects, and demonstration of computer skills. Current students include these elements in their portfolios.

SUMMARY

In summary, the purpose of the employment portfolio is to assist you, the job seeker, in securing employment. But how do you put together an employment portfolio? This book will help you develop one that you can use for the rest of your working life.

The S.T.A.R. Employment Portfolio will help you 'showcase' your S̲kills, T̲raining, A̲ccomplishments, and R̲eferences in order to help you get the job you want. The S.T.A.R. Employment Portfolio is appropriate for any individual to use:

- for all categories of employment including full- and part-time jobs, internships, and co-op experiences
- at any level of education and training, from entry-level and advanced job candidates to mid-life career changers
- with any background and work experience, even if you have little or no work experience

Now turn to Chapter 2 and get started with your own S.T.A.R. Portfolio.

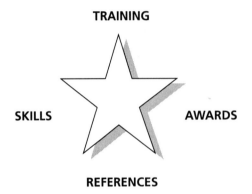

Planning Your Portfolio

Exercises for Creating the S.T.A.R. Portfolio

Identify your ideal job through a description of your primary skills, interests, and career values. Review the following examples, then complete the subsequent exercises.

SKILLS

Check the skills you possess.

■ ADAPTIVE

- _____ accepting criticism
- ___×___ adapting to new or unexpected situations
- ___×___ applying myself to a job without experiencing boredom or distraction
- ___×___ being punctual
- ___×___ being reliable
- ___×___ being responsible
- ___×___ cooperating with others to complete a task

- ___×___ functioning with people whose views differ from my own
- ___×___ learning new things and skills
- ___×___ maintaining a neat attire and personal appearance
- ___×___ taking initiative and working on my own
- _____ working under pressure without becoming upset
- _____ _____

■ CLERICAL/FINANCIAL

- _____ accounting
- _____ attending to details
- _____ bookkeeping
- ___×___ budgeting
- ___×___ editing others' writing
- _____ financing

- _____ fundraising
- _____ keying data into a computer
- _____ recording inventory
- _____ taking messages
- _____ word processing
- _____ _____

7

■ **CONCEPTUAL**

___X___ debating

___X___ organizing ideas

___X___ planning events

___X___ problem solving

___X___ reading and doing research

___X___ studying a favorite subject

___X___ thinking

___X___ writing

_____ _____

■ **CREATIVE**

_____ acting

___X___ cooking

_____ designing things

_____ drawing

_____ playing a musical instrument

_____ singing

_____ writing stories, poems, or plays

_____ _____

■ **MANUAL**

_____ assembling things

_____ athletics

_____ landscaping

_____ participating in sports

_____ raising crops

_____ repairing things

_____ working with animals

_____ working with electricity

_____ working with engines

_____ working with machines

_____ working with metal

_____ working with tools

_____ working with wood

_____ _____

■ **PEOPLE INTERACTION**

___X___ advising

_____ caring for others

_____ complimenting others

___X___ counseling

_____ giving reports

_____ giving tours

___X___ influencing others

___X___ listening to others

_____ making friends easily

___X___ negotiating

_____ selling new products or ideas

___X___ speaking before a group

_____ supervising others

_____ talking with friends

___X___ teaching

_____ volunteering

_____ _____

■ **SCIENTIFIC**

_____ analyzing data

_____ conducting experiments

_____ following directions

_____ learning new technologies

_____ working in teams

_____ _____

INTERESTS

Check what you enjoy or would enjoy.

_____ acting	_____ playing a musical instrument
_____ attending school	__×__ public speaking
_____ boating	_____ putting together puzzles
__×__ camping	_____ raising animals
_____ carpentry	_____ reading
_____ collecting things	_____ refinishing furniture
__×__ cooking	_____ shopping
_____ decorating	_____ singing
__×__ doing research	__×__ talking to people
_____ drawing	__×__ team sports
_____ experimenting	_____ thinking
_____ games	_____ visiting friends
__×__ gardening	__×__ walking/hiking
_____ individual sports	_____ word processing
__×__ interviewing	_____ working with computers
_____ learning foreign languages	_____ working with numbers
_____ making crafts	__×__ writing
_____ participating in clubs	_____ _____
_____ photography	_____ _____

CAREER VALUES

Check the following career values according to the significance each has for you.

	ESSENTIAL	SIGNIFICANT	INSIGNIFICANT
accomplishment	×		
achievement		×	
authority			×
belonging			×
challenge		×	
competence	×		
competition			×
contribution	×		
control			×
creativity		×	
esteem		×	
flexibility		×	
income		×	

(continued)

	ESSENTIAL	SIGNIFICANT	INSIGNIFICANT
independence	×		
influence		×	
money		×	
order		×	
peace of mind		×	
power			×
prestige		×	
recognition		×	
responsibility		×	
security		×	
service to others		×	
status		×	
structure		×	
variety		×	
wealth			×

WORK SETTING PREFERENCE

Check your level of preference for each work setting.

WORK SETTING	+2	+1	0	−1
visible signs of accomplishment	×			
work at an average, natural pace		×		
work at a high-pressure, competitive pace				×
work at a routine, repetitive task				×
work by self			×	
work for large organization/company			×	
work for self		×		
work for small organization/company		×		
work in large group			×	
work in small group		×		
work in warm, caring environment		×		
work indoors		×		
work long hours/overtime		×		
work outside			×	
work regular hours			×	
work with close supervision			×	
work with little or no supervision	×			

IDEAL JOB

■ **SKILLS:**

taking initiative and working on my own

problem solving

influencing others

listening to others

speaking before a group

■ **INTERESTS:**

doing research

interviewing

public speaking

talking to people

writing

■ **VALUES:**

accomplishment

competence

contribution

creativity

independence

■ **COMPLETE:**

My ideal daily activities would consist of:

Interviewing people regarding their problems; analyzing,

researching, and developing solutions that I would present

to individuals or groups.

My participation would serve to improve methods and outcomes.

I could accomplish this in the setting of:

an office, public forum, or information resource center.

WHAT IS YOUR IDEAL JOB?

Now it's your turn. Fill in your answers.

SKILLS

Check the skills you possess.

■ ADAPTIVE

_____ accepting criticism

_____ adapting to new or unexpected situations

_____ applying myself to a job without experiencing boredom or distraction

_____ being punctual

_____ being reliable

_____ being responsible

_____ cooperating with others to complete a task

_____ functioning with people whose views differ from my own

_____ learning new things and skills

_____ maintaining a neat attire and personal appearance

_____ taking initiative and working on my own

_____ working under pressure without becoming upset

_____ _____

■ CLERICAL/FINANCIAL

_____ accounting

_____ attending to details

_____ bookkeeping

_____ budgeting

_____ editing others' writing

_____ financing

_____ fundraising

_____ keying data into a computer

_____ recording inventory

_____ taking messages

_____ word processing

_____ _____

■ CONCEPTUAL

_____ debating

_____ organizing ideas

_____ planning events

_____ problem solving

_____ reading and doing research

_____ studying a favorite subject

_____ thinking

_____ writing

_____ _____

■ CREATIVE

_____ acting

_____ cooking

_____ designing things

_____ drawing

_____ playing a musical instrument

_____ singing

_____ writing stories, poems, or plays

_____ _____

■ MANUAL

_____ assembling things

_____ athletics

_____ landscaping

_____ participating in sports

_____ raising crops

_____ repairing things

_____ working with animals

_____ working with electricity

_____ working with engines
_____ working with machines
_____ working with metal

_____ working with tools
_____ working with wood
_____ _____

■ **PEOPLE INTERACTION**

_____ advising
_____ caring for others
_____ complimenting others
_____ counseling
_____ giving reports
_____ giving tours
_____ influencing others
_____ listening to others
_____ making friends easily

_____ negotiating
_____ selling new products or ideas
_____ speaking before a group
_____ supervising others
_____ talking with friends
_____ teaching
_____ volunteering
_____ _____

■ **SCIENTIFIC**

_____ analyzing data
_____ conducting experiments
_____ following directions

_____ learning new technologies
_____ working in teams
_____ _____

INTERESTS

Check what you enjoy or would enjoy.

_____ acting
_____ attending school
_____ boating
_____ camping
_____ carpentry
_____ collecting things
_____ cooking
_____ decorating
_____ doing research
_____ drawing
_____ experimenting
_____ games
_____ gardening
_____ individual sports
_____ interviewing
_____ learning foreign languages
_____ making crafts
_____ participating in clubs
_____ photography

_____ playing a musical instrument
_____ public speaking
_____ putting together puzzles
_____ raising animals
_____ reading
_____ refinishing furniture
_____ shopping
_____ singing
_____ talking to people
_____ team sports
_____ thinking
_____ visiting friends
_____ walking/hiking
_____ word processing
_____ working with computers
_____ working with numbers
_____ writing
_____ _____
_____ _____

CAREER VALUES

Check the following career values according to the significance each has for you.

	ESSENTIAL	SIGNIFICANT	INSIGNIFICANT
accomplishment			
achievement			
authority			
belonging			
challenge			
competence			
competition			
contribution			
control			
creativity			
esteem			
flexibility			
income			
independence			
influence			
money			
order			
peace of mind			
power			
prestige			
recognition			
responsibility			
security			
service to others			
status			
structure			
variety			
wealth			

WORK SETTING PREFERENCE

WORK SETTING	+2	+1	0	−1
visible signs of accomplishment				
work at an average, natural pace				
work at a high-pressure, competitive pace				
work at a routine, repetitive task				
work by self				
work for large organization/company				
work for self				
work for small organization/company				
work in large group				
work in small group				
work in warm, caring environment				
work indoors				
work long hours/overtime				
work outside				
work regular hours				
work with close supervision				
work with little or no supervision				

IDEAL JOB

List your five key skills, interests, and career values. Reference your checklists when necessary.

■ **SKILLS:**

_____

_____

_____

_____

_____

■ **INTERESTS:**

_____

_____

_____

_____

_____

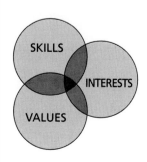

(continued)

■ **VALUES:**

_____

_____

_____

_____

_____

■ **COMPLETE** (emphasizing the intersection of your skills, interests, and career values):

My ideal daily activities would consist of:

_____

_____

_____

_____

_____

_____

I could accomplish this in the setting of:

_____

_____

Check your level of preference for each work setting.

If you have completely and successfully described your ideal job, you are ready to proceed. If you have not, you should consult with your career counselor, who can help you identify your skills, interests, and career values and refine them through testing, interviewing, and counseling.

PHILOSOPHY OF WORK

What is your philosophy of work? Through review of the ideal job exercises, careful thought, and reflection, compose your philosophy of work. The person who filled out the ideal job sample composed the following philosophy of work.

"My philosophy of work is one in which I work with a small group of people in a team effort. I believe in contributing to the greater good. By doing this I hope to model behavior for co-workers who hopefully will show or will adopt a cooperative process. I nevertheless am willing to initiate activities necessary to more efficiently meet goals. I seek to influence others and to positively improve clients' outlook and outcomes. I find that working as a team with each person, having specific responsibilities, expectations, and authority to implement, and working toward a described goal, allows me to be most productive and fulfilled. I work to achieve goals, impact change, and identify accomplishments."

In the box, describe your philosophy of work as reflected in your skills, interests, values, and work setting preferences.

My philosophy of work is:

_____

_____

_____

_____

Consult individuals who know you and whose judgment you trust. Request constructive critiques. Review your statement in light of short- and long-term goals. Revise and rewrite.

My philosophy of work is:

■ **SHORT-TERM GOALS:**

_____

_____

_____

_____

■ **LONG-TERM GOALS:**

_____

_____

_____

_____

DEVELOPING THE COMPONENTS OF THE S.T.A.R. EMPLOYMENT PORTFOLIO

You are now ready to develop the four components (Skills, Training, Accomplishments/ Awards, and References) of your S.T.A.R. Employment Portfolio.

SKILLS

Most jobs require many diversified skills. The better you can identify and verbalize your skills, the greater is your likelihood of securing meaningful employment. From the list appearing earlier in the chapter and from the following list, copy the skills that most characterize your skills on the job or at your ideal job.

PARTIAL LIST OF SKILLS

Accounting skills	Legal skills
Animal services skills	Managerial skills
Art skills	Manual skills
Building skills	Marketing/advertising skills
Business skills	Mathematical skills
Communication skills	Mechanical skills
Computer skills	Medical skills
Counseling skills	Motivational skills
Craft skills	Music skills
Crisis management skills	Negotiating skills
Culinary skills	Office skills
Customer service skills	Organizational skills
Decorating skills	People skills
Design skills	Physical skills
Drawing skills	Remodeling skills
Engineering skills	Research skills
Exercise skills	Sales skills
Farming/horticultural skills	Science skills
Financial skills	Speaking skills
Fundraising skills	Sports skills
Game skills	Technical skills
Graphic skills	Telemarketing skills
Group skills	Training skills
Journalism skills	Typing skills
Keyboarding skills	Word-processing skills
Laboring skills	Writing skills

■ **DETAILED SKILLS (EXAMPLES)**

1. make independent judgments based upon investigation and analysis and initiate a reasonable course of action
2. solve problems through objectives and logical thought based in experience, information, and sound judgment
3. influence others through convincing and persuasive arguments
4. gain insight into the nature of a problem through earnest and active listening
5. speak before small and large groups in an informative, humorous, and persuasive fashion

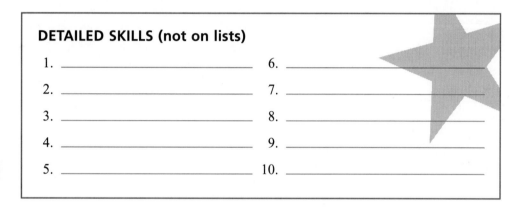

TEN GENERAL SKILLS (from lists)

1. _____ 6. _____
2. _____ 7. _____
3. _____ 8. _____
4. _____ 9. _____
5. _____ 10. _____

Highlight the four skills you most wish to use in a job after listing ten in the box below.

DETAILED SKILLS (not on lists)

1. _____ 6. _____
2. _____ 7. _____
3. _____ 8. _____
4. _____ 9. _____
5. _____ 10. _____

TRAINING

Training refers to formal and/or informal courses, certificates, certifications, licenses, workshops, seminars, or degrees that you have earned or will earn in the near future. Examples of your training allow you to demonstrate to a prospective employer that you have undertaken a rigorous sequence of developmental exercises reflected in written recognition or award for completion, such as a degree or certificate. Here is a partial list of some of the types of training that you might include.

■ **TRAINING**

- Associate degree(s)
- Baccalaureate degree(s)
- Partially completed degree(s)
- Master's degree(s)
- Doctoral degree(s)
- Professional degree(s)
- Certificate(s)
- License(s)
- Certification(s)
- Specific course(s)
- Workshop(s) completed/seminar(s)
- Informal course(s)
- On-the-job training
- Company course(s)

List any training or partial training programs that you have completed. If you have completed a degree or certificate, you do not have to list specific courses included in that program. Listing courses may be helpful, however, if the courses are related to your career goals or a specific job. Fill in the related training areas that you have in the boxes below.

DEGREES

1. _____
2. _____
3. _____
4. _____

CERTIFICATES

1. _____
2. _____
3. _____
4. _____

LICENSES/CERTIFICATIONS (Current or Pending)

1. _____
2. _____
3. _____
4. _____

COURSES/WORKSHOPS/SEMINARS-OJT(On-the-Job Training)

1. _____	7. _____
2. _____	8. _____
3. _____	9. _____
4. _____	10. _____
5. _____	11. _____
6. _____	12. _____

ACCOMPLISHMENTS/AWARDS

Under Accomplishments, list all of your awards and accomplishments, regardless of how insignificant you may think they are. These examples should help you recall some of your accomplishments.

■ **AWARDS/RECOGNITIONS**

- Dean's list
- National dean's list
- Academic honors
- High QPA/GPA
- Scholarships
- Outstanding student/ graduate awards
- Community awards
- Church awards

- Graduation awards
- Athletic awards
- Scholastic awards
- Club/activity awards
- Contest awards
- Work awards, i.e., employee of the month, employee of the year
- Board memberships

■ **ACCOMPLISHMENTS**

- Membership in club/organization
- Officer in club/organization
- Works published
- Course projects
- Work projects
- Coaching achievements
- Athletic achievements
- Military rank
- Participant/presenter/coordinator
- Work promotion

- Testimonials received
- Volunteer service
- Scouting rank
- Elected office(s) held
- Outstanding speech(es) performed
- Outstanding paper(s) delivered
- Board membership
- Patents held
- Creative projects
- Fundraising

List 10 of your accomplishments, awards, and recognitions. List from the most recent to the earliest event.

TOP 10 NOTABLE ACCOMPLISHMENTS

1. _____
2. _____
3. _____
4. _____
5. _____
6. _____
7. _____
8. _____
9. _____
10. _____

If you feel that you cannot fill in the 10 slots, ask your family, friends, teachers, and/or counselors who know you best for feedback in this area. We all have accomplishments in a range between personal to highly recognizable, but most of them are usually somewhere in the middle. Brag a little and make your list.

REFERENCES

References are more than just a list of people that you can give to a prospective employer. References must be carefully planned to deliver the right effect on the potential employer. Include your references in your portfolio but *not* on your resume for the following five reasons:

1. References take up too much space on your resume.
2. You may want to change references depending on the job for which you apply.
3. You might develop new references, such as a new teacher, employer, or supervisor on your co-op, internship, or clinical.
4. You may choose to bring references to the employer on another day; this amounts to a *second interview.* Use this technique only if enough time is available or if you are one of the first candidates interviewed.
5. Have a page of references prepared for your interview in case the employer needs one immediately. Take one with you on all interviews.

Here are four different types of S.T.A.R. Portfolio references that you might use.

■ FOUR TYPES OF PORTFOLIO REFERENCES

- Letters of reference (recommendations and descriptions of skills from employers, employees, and colleagues)
- Letters of commendation (letters of appreciation, recognition, praise, or thanks for a particular service or accomplishment)
- Letters of introduction (personal references from friends, neighbors, community members, faculty, employers, or acquaintances)
- Letters of personal reference (recommendations concerning your loyalty, dedication, integrity, character, personality, and community involvement)

Type your references onto a page headed with your name, address, and phone number. List at least three references, including names, positions, places and addresses of employment, and phone numbers. Remember, your references may change with the particular job for which you are applying. List five references for your reference page, including each person's relationship to you, such as instructor, clinical supervisor, work supervisor, or colleague. Use *only* three references when you prepare the final reference sheet for each job interview.

5 REFERENCES FOR MY PORTFOLIO

1. Name _____

   Title _____

   Employer _____

   Address _____

   City/State/Zip _____

   Phone No. ( ) _____

   Fax No. ( ) _____ E-mail _____

2. Name _____

   Title _____

   Employer _____

   Address _____

   City/State/Zip _____

   Phone No. (   ) _____

   Fax No. (   )   E-mail _____

3. Name _____

   Title _____

   Employer _____

   Address _____

   City/State/Zip _____

   Phone No. (   ) _____

   Fax No. (   )   E-mail _____

4. Name _____

   Title _____

   Employer _____

   Address _____

   City/State/Zip _____

   Phone No. (   ) _____

   Fax No. (   )   E-mail _____

5. Name _____

   Title _____

   Employer _____

   Address _____

   City/State/Zip _____

   Phone No. (   ) _____

   Fax No. (   )   E-mail _____

Now that you have your formal references in place, list any other people, customers' letters, notes of thanks, and letters from employers that you can use to project to prospective employers the type of person and team player you are. List at least five of these in your portfolio that you might use or be prepared to ask for in the future.

Reference Name/Phone	Corresponding Document
1. _____	_____
_____	_____
_____	_____
2. _____	_____
_____	_____
_____	_____
3. _____	_____
_____	_____
_____	_____
4. _____	_____
_____	_____
_____	_____
5. _____	_____
_____	_____
_____	_____

Producing a special letter of accomplishment from your portfolio at the right moment during the interview provides supporting documentation in your favor. It shows not only that others commend you, but that you are well organized, prepared, and communicate competently. You will sparkle with this S.T.A.R. approach.

WORKSHEET FOR YOUR S.T.A.R. EMPLOYMENT PORTFOLIO

Fill in the spaces in the worksheet provided. This page will be the start of your "Table of Contents" for your portfolio. Treat this exercise as a brainstorming session, listing as many of your significant and relevant skills that pertain to the job as possible. Do the same for Training, Accomplishments, and References. Refer to all of the earlier sections of this chapter that you have completed. Make copies of this page so you can:

PHILOSOPHY OF WORK

Indeed it is of the essence of man . . . that he can lose himself in the jungle of his existence, within himself, and thanks to his sensation of being lost can react by setting energetically to work to find himself again.

JOSE ORTEGA Y GASSET

1. Apply for different types of jobs using a variation of your S.T.A.R. Employment Portfolio.
2. Have more lists than one page will hold. Remember to list all your relevant qualities.
3. Have a teacher, friend, family member, former employer, or colleague complete a page for you. You may discover many accomplishments and skills that you overlooked. Their insight may be very useful in compiling your portfolio.
4. Summarize all of your worksheets together on one page.

WORKSHEET FOR YOUR S. T. A. R. PORTFOLIO

COLLEGE MAJOR:

OBJECTIVE:

■ **SKILLS**

1. _____

2. _____

3. _____

4. _____

5. _____

■ **TRAINING**

1. _____

2. _____

3. _____

4. _____

5. _____

■ **ACCOMPLISHMENTS**

1. _____

2. _____

3. _____

4. _____

5. _____

■ **REFERENCES**

1. _____

2. _____

3. _____

4. _____

5. _____

SEVEN TIPS FOR DEVELOPING YOUR S.T.A.R. EMPLOYMENT PORTFOLIO

TIP 1: SELECT A COLLABORATOR

Think of three people who could collaborate with you to develop your portfolio. One collaborator may help you create the S.T.A.R. Portfolio and another may help you prepare the presentation and delivery of your documents.

Select Collaborators such as a friend, employer, advisor, parent, teacher, fellow employee, spouse, or mentor to help you choose specific documents for your presentation. Your collaborator(s) should be knowledgeable persons who will give you honest, sincere, and constructive feedback on what should and should not go into your portfolio. Set up regular times to meet with your collaborator(s), such as once a week for three weeks. Your collaborator(s) will be a tremendous help not only in assisting you in putting together your portfolio but in helping you simulate the presentation of your portfolio in preparation for an actual job interview. Practice, practice, and continue to practice your presentation to achieve perfection, enthusiasm, and naturalness.

List three collaborators, their titles, and how they can help you develop and present your portfolio to your next employer.

YOUR COLLABORATORS

	Name	Job Title	Assistance
1.			
2.			
3.			

Ask your collaborators to assist you in three ways: (1) in your job search, (2) in the development, and (3) in the presentation of your S.T.A.R. EMPLOYMENT PORTFOLIO. Seek their advice, but make selections for your portfolio that you will feel comfortable presenting to an employer.

TIP 2: ORGANIZE YOUR PORTFOLIO

Organize your portfolio in a style that others can easily follow with contents grouped under specific job requirements using skills, training, accomplishments, and references. Create a Table of Contents.

Sally, a nontraditional associate degree graduate, age 33, majored in accounting. She prepared her portfolio using a loose-leaf binder with each document placed in a non-glare plastic page cover. She also had a large document that she used as a sample of her work that was not part of her binder. Sally used a professional leather attaché case that she bought at a local office supply store to carry her binder, resume, references, cover letter, and the large samples of her work. She made the right impression and got the job!

Evan Macovich, a history professor with years of experience, applied for a professorship using a folder file portfolio that he carried in his briefcase. Whenever his review committee could benefit from documentation, he reached into his briefcase and retrieved an appropriate document to strengthen and justify what he was saying through a direct illustration of his work, an analysis of his writing, or student feedback. He was prepared and was promoted to a full professor based upon his accomplishments, which he documented at the interview through the use of his portfolio.

The ways your S.T.A.R. Employment Portfolio may be organized varies with your presentation. Here are various forms of organization you might use:

- loose-leaf binder (preferably with a zipper closure)
- bound binder
- separate pages
- videotape
- audiotape
- photo album
- internet Web site(s)
- computer disk
- overheads, slides, presentation software

What are some ways you want to use to put together your portfolio?

PORTFOLIO FORMS I CAN USE

	Type	Reason
1.	_____	_____
2.	_____	_____
3.	_____	_____
4.	_____	_____

THREE PATHS TO A PROFESSIONAL PORTFOLIO

1. Reference your portfolio in your cover letter. Attach your Table of Contents or include a disk of your portfolio with your cover letter. This is particularly effective when communicating with small companies or arranging for informational interviews. Put your portfolio on the Web.
2. Make it look professionally prepared. Go to a print shop or use a desktop publishing program.
3. Have your collaborator(s) assess your portfolio. Make sure they give you honest feedback.

TIP 3: BE PROFESSIONAL

If you are preparing the portfolio for a job search, it should present your best attributes in a quality format. It must be neat, clean, concise, and cogent. Create your portfolio on a state-of-the-art word processor and print it on a laser printer, or take it to a professional printing establishment. This is where your collaborator can help you with feedback on the exact impression it will make on the interviewer. Your portfolio is a reflection of you as a professional.

TIP 4: ASSESS YOUR S.T.A.R. EMPLOYMENT PORTFOLIO

Assess your portfolio for two types of applications: (1) for an individual, one-on-one interview and (2) for a group interview. Arrange your portfolio according to what topics and subjects you want to bring up with this particular employer. Your portfolio must be fluid because it changes with each type of job and interview. You may want to use certain documents with this interview and certain other documents with others. Organize your documents into the categories of the job description. This approach is another way in which you can develop, arrange, and showcase your portfolio in terms of assessing what you need for a particular interview. Do not clutter your portfolio. Be relevant, be specific, and be direct.

Fill in three ways to assess your portfolio:

1. _____

2. _____

3. _____

TIP 5: BE TIMELY ON THE PRESENTATION OF YOUR PORTFOLIO

Go with the flow. If your interview leads you to a point where your portfolio can be an asset, use it. Comedian Bob Hope once said "Timing is everything." His impeccable timing, however, came through years of practice. His timing seemed so natural, so unpracticed. This tip on timing must be practiced so that you are using your portfolio in your job presentation just as Mr. Hope uses his delivery in telling a joke or a line in a story.

Norman Rockwell received $500,000 for a poster he created in 30 minutes. When someone asked him if the money seemed excessive, Mr. Rockwell replied that it had taken him 35 years of practice to produce the drawing that he just effortlessly sketched in only 30 minutes. His practice, discipline, and adherence to his goal kept him on track in his artwork. Use your portfolio with proper timing acquired through practice, using well-prepared documents that illustrate what you can do for the employer.

TIP 6: FIELD-TEST YOUR PORTFOLIO IN ACTUAL INTERVIEWS WITH EMPLOYERS

Choose several jobs out of the newspaper, employment office, or college placement office. Choose jobs that are somewhat lower than your expectations, but ones in which you can use your portfolio presentation.

Now present your portfolio for three reasons: (1) in an attempt to have the employer consider you for a higher level position; (2) to have the employer remember you favorably for employment; and (3) to field test your portfolio.

This approach reduces your stress because of your portfolio. You may even get a job offer. If the employer is advertising for a lower level job, there may be several other job openings that are higher paying with more challenging work assignments. But you are under no pressure at this time. Relax and let the portfolio guide you through the interview process. At this point you have practiced interviewing with your collaborator; you are well prepared. Take a deep breath, relax, and prepare to get the job offer.

List five employers with whom you can interview who have actual job openings in your career field. Call them for a job interview.

Name	Phone/E-mail	Company
1.		
2.		
3.		
4.		
5.		

PRACTICE • TIMING • PRACTICE

NOTES: How to Improve My Portfolio Presentation

Compliments	Areas in Need of Improvement

JOB INTERVIEWING SKILLS MAKE YOU A STAR

You are just starting. Make the improvements and move on to your next interview.

TIP 7: FOCUS ON YOUR S.T.A.R. EMPLOYMENT PORTFOLIO

Prepare to focus on the interviewer's points to answer specific questions such as, "What was your greatest accomplishment on your last job (or in school)?" Draw from your portfolio file a document that shows your accomplishments on your current or last job. Indicate specific plans or strategies to respond to the question. With the help of the S.T.A.R. Employment Portfolio, you will appear focused, enthusiastic, and accomplished. Again, FOCUS stands for:

Framing the question to use with your portfolio

Opportunity for demonstrating your skills and abilities

Creating a plan to use your portfolio's references

Understanding the nature of the new job

Strengthening your position by enthusiastically demonstrating your accomplishments

When playing tennis, you must follow the ball. When you see the ball strike your racquet, you follow through. Michael Jordan said on a TV interview that the quick movement on the basketball court seems to slow down and he sees everything moving in slow motion. His mind is racing ahead. He sees his shot before he takes it. His visualization and follow-through have helped him become the greatest player in the game. He is totally focused. We, too, can become better players with the follow-through by using our S.T.A.R. Employment Portfolio. Remember to stay focused on each question with an answer that has good follow-through.

How to Use the S.T.A.R. Portfolio to Get the Interview and the Job

In Chapter 2, we learned how to write a Table of Contents for our S.T.A.R. Portfolio and how to assemble the portfolio for presentation. Let us review the seven tips for developing your S.T.A.R. Portfolio.

Much of your work has now been completed through these seven tips. Tip 3 advised "Be professional." Being professional begins with appearing professional. Use this advice in your cover letter, in your Table of Contents, and on your job interview. Let others see your professionalism every day that you are searching for a job, at your place of employment, or in dealing with your colleagues outside of work. The S.T.A.R. Portfolio will help you in two ways. First, the Table of Contents of the S.T.A.R. Portfolio can help you get the job you want, and second, it can help you plan for your next job. As Tip 5 points out, you must be timely on your presentation of your portfolio's contents, which can only be accomplished through practice and hard work. "Genius is 99% perspiration and only 1% inspiration," observed Thomas Edison. Now the perspiration will continue until you have the job of your dreams.

> ## 7 TIPS FOR DEVELOPING YOUR S.T.A.R. PORTFOLIO
>
> 1. Select a collaborator
> 2. Organize your portfolio
> 3. Be professional
> 4. Assess your S.T.A.R. employment portfolio
> 5. Be timely on the presentation of your portfolio
> 6. Field-test your portfolio in actual interviews with employers
> 7. Focus on your S.T.A.R. employment portfolio

GETTING THE JOB INTERVIEW WITH THE HELP OF THE S.T.A.R. PORTFOLIO

There are three main approaches when using the S.T.A.R. Portfolio to help you get the job interview. These approaches are:

1. Attach your S.T.A.R. Portfolio "Table of Contents" to your resume.
2. Refer to the S.T.A.R. Portfolio when you are talking to an employer on the telephone, or voice mail.
3. Attach samples of the S.T.A.R. Portfolio to your cover letter.

A. FIRST APPROACH: USING THE TABLE OF CONTENTS

John Joseph was a senior at a large university in New York. He was graduating in May, just 2 months away, and needed an excellent cover letter to set him apart from every other graduate in the paralegal field. John knew through his self-assessment of his own skills, training, accomplishments, and references that he was a superior candidate for a paralegal job. Not only did the S.T.A.R. Portfolio show him that he was well prepared to look for paralegal work but it also gave him the confidence to conduct a first-class job search. John wrote his S.T.A.R. Table of Contents before he put together his S.T.A.R. Portfolio. Afterward, he had to revise his Table of Contents for each job for which he applied. With his improved Table of Contents for his S.T.A.R. Portfolio, John referred to it in his cover letter and sent a copy of two reference letters along with his resume. John explained how the S.T.A.R. Portfolio would demonstrate to the employer that his skills, training, and accomplishments would make him an outstanding candidate for the job. His professional references would help verify and strengthen his portfolio. By using this method, John expanded his accomplishments via his cover letters and landed six job interviews. He received four job offers. John claims that his S.T.A.R. Portfolio helped him get the interview and then the job. The S.T.A.R. Portfolio gave John the edge he needed to get the interviews.

JOHN JOSEPH'S COVER LETTER

West 88th Street, S519
New York, New York 10024
August 15, 1999

John Hayes, Esquire
Smith, Hayes, & Burns, Law Firm
1011 Grant Street
Pittsburgh, PA 15221

Dear Mr. Hayes:

I have been referred to you by Attorney Bill Zonick from the firm of Zonick and Tucker in New York City in regard to a possible paralegal position with your law firm in Pittsburgh.

I am very much interested in the position since I am returning to Pittsburgh to live on a permanent basis. I completed my Paralegal Certificate with a 4.0 QPA from Community College of Allegheny County before earning a B.A. in Legal Studies at Columbia University. While at Columbia I maintained a 3.6 QPA in all my courses and graduated with honors. In addition, I enhanced my studies by completing internships at two law firms during my junior and senior years.

I know that your firm specializes in estates and trust planning. I have a particular interest in this area since I set up a computer program for estates and trusts particularly for Attorney Zonick. He thought the program improved his ability to deal with clients more effectively and efficiently, thus saving time and money. My internship with him in my senior year not only was an excellent learning experience for me in estates and trust, but also a permanent improvement to the firm in delivery of services to clients.

Enclosed is a copy of my resume and letter of reference from Attorney Zonick documenting my skills and accomplishments. You can locate my complete employment portfolio, including the estate and trusts software demonstration, on my Web page at www.unix1.columbia.jjoseph.edu.

Please contact me by phone or e-mail before September 14 to set up an interview. I am looking forward to meeting you.

Sincerely,

John Joseph

Let us review the steps John used. First he thoroughly developed and revised his portfolio and Table of Contents. Secondly he incorporated parts of his S.T.A.R. Portfolio into his cover letter. In fact the S.T.A.R. Portfolio helped him organize his cover letter:

JOHN JOSEPH'S OUTLINE FOR HIS COVER LETTER:

1. Told why he was writing the letter—to apply for a particular job opening
2. Wrote about his skills particular to the job
3. Described his training and accomplishments
4. Mentioned his S.T.A.R. Portfolio
5. Referred to his references and resume
6. Asked for an interview
7. Enclosed his resume and S.T.A.R. Portfolio Table of Contents

John's outline for his cover letter sounds simple, straightforward, and easy to write. The letter, however, took hours of preparation and hard work in building his special S.T.A.R. Portfolio for this job. Once the portfolio was completed, the cover letter and the job interview were, as John described them, "easier than I thought." The first approach shows you how to use your S.T.A.R. Portfolio to organize and write your cover letter. Mention the S.T.A.R. Portfolio and the items included, such as the references that you are going to bring with you to the job interview. Be professional, neat, and smooth in your approach.

> ## B. REFER TO THE S.T.A.R. PORTFOLIO TABLE OF CONTENTS WHEN YOU ARE TALKING TO THE EMPLOYER ON THE PHONE

Every good job seeker knows that every personal contact with an employer is a job interview. This contact can be over the phone or in person. A communication company once hired a high level director through a group interview, but this candidate was interviewed only over the phone! She got the job. The important point to remember is that even the telephone inquiry to the employer is in fact a job interview.

PART-TIME EMPLOYMENT

Susan Hayward, a 32-year-old married mother, was looking for a part-time job so she could raise her two children. The job had to pay enough to offset the baby-sitting fees and be of sufficient interest to keep her intellectually stimulated and happy. Susan was continuing her education, majoring in accounting at a local community college. She knew she was doing well at school even though her first impression was one of awe. She was not sure of herself when she started, but after a few courses she set her career goals even higher. She wanted to earn her C.P.A., her Certified Public Accounting license, from the state. She also knew that any relevant experience was going to help her understand what accountants actually did on the job, which would make her education even more relevant and meaningful. Here is how she accomplished this feat.

First, she made a list of all her contacts. She called them and was able to use their names as references when she contacted local C.P.A. firms. Second, she called the C.P.A. firms, mentioning her references and then her skills, which were listed on her S.T.A.R. Portfolio Table of Contents. She knew her skills were all in order and well documented in her portfolio. She did not hesitate to describe briefly some of her skills and then her training over the phone. Finally she mentioned a few of her accomplishments. She impressed an employer with her sincerity and enthusiasm. She asked if she could come into the office to speak to them about accounting careers, including C.P.A. credentials. She mentioned over the phone that she would be bringing a copy of her portfolio to give to the employer. The portfolio also included her resume. Of course, everything in the S.T.A.R. Portfolio presented the best picture of herself to the employer for this particular job. She copied the pages on good-quality paper, bound them in a clear plastic cover, and created a cover page: The S.T.A.R. Portfolio of Susan J. Hayward.

Susan inserted her resume immediately after the cover page. Even the resume was built around her skills, training, accomplishments, and references. All of these followed as small headings listed on her resume. The results of her job preparation were impressive. She asked for the job and received an offer with more money than she originally had thought possible. She was excited that she now had an opportunity to work within her field of study and interest. She worked hard for this opportunity, which paid off in a big way. Now it was up to her to prove to herself and to her employer that she could do the job in a quick, efficient, and capable manner.

See the box for a review of Susan's seven steps to a job using her S.T.A.R. Portfolio.

SEVEN STEPS TO SUSAN'S JOB OFFER

1. Listed potential contacts who might know someone working in a C.P.A. firm
2. Contacted C.P.A. firms using her networking contacts and references
3. Stated her skills, training, and accomplishments
4. Set up interviews to discuss accounting careers
5. Compiled a customized S.T.A.R. Portfolio for each prospective employer
6. Interviewed prospective employers, presenting to each a customized copy of her S.T.A.R. Portfolio
7. Asked for the job

C. ATTACH SAMPLES OF THE S.T.A.R. PORTFOLIO TO YOUR COVER LETTER

Attach samples of the S.T.A.R. Portfolio to your cover letter with every resume you send out to an employer. This means that the cover letter, resume, and samples from your S.T.A.R. Portfolio are printed on good bond paper, preferably white or off-white. Your resume paper and type of print should match your cover letter and envelopes as well as any attached sections from your S.T.A.R. Portfolio.

When Joe Beam finished a master's degree in philosophy, he was 24 years old and unable to obtain a teaching position. He tried looking for a job at major universities in several cities. With the help of his S.T.A.R. Portfolio, he landed a job interview. Here is how Joe got the interview through sending the employer his cover letter, resume, and selections from his S.T.A.R. Portfolio.

Joe wanted to work with people in an academic setting. The job could be teaching or in any support services area related to teaching, such as academic advising. Joe sent in several reference letters from faculty and employers that praised Joe's work as an instructor and as a camp counselor. Working with young people helped Joe mature and build strong personal qualifications, confidence, and character. Joe's reference letters helped him get an interview for the advising job. His references showed that he had excellent skills, including caring and dedication to the service of others. This type of person was exactly who the university was looking for in its advising personnel. The university hired him as an academic advisor and paid for his doctorate, which he completed. Joe was lucky, yes. But he was also prepared and used his S.T.A.R. Portfolio, from which he selected those documents that he felt would give him a better chance of being contacted for a job interview. His hard work paid off with a good job at a main university close to Joe's home in Boston.

Jill Jackson was 35 years old, single, and open to travel. She wanted a job that was exciting and filled with new challenges. She also wanted a job that paid more money than she was making. Jill felt that her current position was as high as she could go in the organization. She had hit the so-called "glass ceiling." Her current position was director of public relations at a medium-sized manufacturing company. She was finding that her personal budget was very tight. After she paid for her apartment, car, food, clothes, utilities, insurance, and entertainment, there was little left for savings or vacation. In short, she needed more money to do the things she always wanted to do.

She researched the job market in order to explore possible positions. She decided on a computer service area to explore with several companies. From her contacts with local organizations, the employers there knew she was well liked and perceived as a hard worker. What they did not know about were her qualifications, skills, and accomplishments in the computer field. From Jill's S.T.A.R. Portfolio she selected several computer projects and competencies that were well thought of and praised, as stated clearly through letters from her supervisors and the company president. She faxed copies of these letters plus her computerized projects to the companies on her contact list. She then followed up with hard copies in color with a request from her to meet with each employer to explain these projects in more detail. Several companies invited her in to present her projects. To her surprise, they considered this the best form of job interviewing because she would be making presentations all over the United States.

They were impressed with her enthusiasm, perseverance, and professionalism. She received several job offers. Now she has money to save and is traveling to new and exciting places. She started by formulating and putting together her S.T.A.R. Portfolio, which gave her the confidence and direction to pursue other career options based on her current background. She did not need additional training, but she did need to do a lot of preparing to set her new sights through developing her S.T.A.R. Portfolio. She had time to think and plan her best strategies for today and tomorrow. Jill continues to keep her portfolio updated because she may change jobs in the future. Her S.T.A.R. Portfolio is developing and changing with all her additional accomplishments, skill development, and on-the-job training. She knows that her S.T.A.R. Portfolio is ready and waiting if and when she needs to use it for her next job adventure.

> **RESEARCH THE JOB MARKET** using the Internet, library, and Personal Contacts.

CONCLUSION

There are myriad ways to use the S.T.A.R. Portfolio to obtain a job interview. Be creative, be prepared, and be professional. The S.T.A.R. Portfolio will guide you along the way as you reach for your next dream job. Be a true self-promoter through your S.T.A.R. Portfolio.

HOW TO USE YOUR S.T.A.R. PORTFOLIO ON THE JOB INTERVIEW

Once you have a job interview, you are now ready to focus in on your S.T.A.R. Portfolio. Your Portfolio will guide you in presenting visual documentation of your entire work experience and background. Your assembled S.T.A.R. Portfolio for a particular job interview is carefully selected from your main S.T.A.R. Portfolio, copied, and placed in an attractive clear plastic case with a cover page identifying your portfolio. For example,

1. Nursing Career Portfolio for James Smith
2. Accounting Portfolio for Joseph W. Jones
3. The Job Portfolio of Thomas Block
4. Portfolio of Thomas Block for the Mechanical Engineering Position at USX
5. Just your name, centered and neatly typed as below:

Thomas J. Block, R.N.

You can use your S.T.A.R. Portfolio for every interview. If you are applying for different types of positions, select only the pertinent information for each job for which you are applying. Yes, it is hard work. But you have done the hardest part, which is getting the job interview. Now is the time for an all-out preparation for the job interview.

> **THE S.T.A.R. PORTFOLIO REPRESENTS YOU—** Be focused and professional.

TEN INTERVIEW QUESTIONS AND HOW TO ANSWER THEM
USING YOUR S.T.A.R. PORTFOLIO

Now you have several interviews. How do you use your portfolio to your best advantage? As always, you must make a good first impression to interest the employer in you as a candidate for the job. First impressions are lasting. Next the interviewer will be asking you questions to uncover your skills, training, aptitudes, attitudes, personality, and communication strengths. In short, the employer will be interviewing you to judge whether you would be the best person for this job opening. For each question asked, the experienced interviewer has a specific reason on his or her mind. Some reasons for the question might be to discover maturity level, organizational ability, skill level, logic, team play, speaking ability, and leadership qualities, to name a few. You should concentrate not only on answering the question but also showing the employer you know the reasons why the question was asked. You can now give a better answer with a fuller understanding of the question. You in turn will use your S.T.A.R. Portfolio to guide you through the interviewing process by placing each question under Skills, Training, Accomplishments, and/or References. This outline will help you understand why the employer is asking the question and will give you a simple and direct reply based on the employer's needs. This outline seems at times too simple. DO NOT read too deeply into each question. The employer wants to hear how you can make his or her business or company more productive and prosperous. Using the S.T.A.R. Portfolio as a guideline will help you do your best to get the job and make a lasting impression with your closing or summary at the end of your interview.

■ QUESTION 1

The first question, and one that is asked in many interviews, is **"Tell me about yourself,"** or **"Tell me why you applied for this job."** This is an open-ended question that has no particular answer. The employer is looking for logic, organization, and relevancy; in short, how you can help the employer and the company. You must be succinct. "Don't talk too much" is rule number one. Rule number two is "don't talk too little." Answer each question with a complete sentence.

This question, "Tell me about yourself," is a difficult question to answer effectively, but by using the S.T.A.R. Portfolio as a guide, you will be a "pro." Here is a typical response that you might use, showcasing your portfolio. "Let me tell you about my training, skills, and accomplishments." Or "First I will discuss my educational background and training, and then my relevant experience and skills." In either case, you have a perfect opportunity to organize your answer, and be logical and relevant, using <u>S</u>kills, <u>T</u>raining, <u>A</u>ccomplishments, and <u>R</u>eferences. You will have the perfect answer to this open-ended question.

■ QUESTION 2

Another difficult question to answer is **"Can you describe several of your main accomplishments?"** Most people do not want to brag or boast about their achievements. Others are not prepared for this question. You will plan a strategy to respond with a coherent answer backed up with documentation on your achievements, awards, and accomplishments. You will make a very good impression by producing a sample of your work or a letter of recommendation documenting the success of your particular project. For example, one salesperson stated that one of his main accomplishments was winning the "Sales Representative of the Year" award. He then described how he had accomplished this and how he had attracted a large number of new clients. He then produced from his portfolio the "Sales Award Certificate" and a letter of praise from a vice president of one of his larger accounts. He made a great impression on the employer. He sold himself through his portfolio.

Another example is from an accountant named Bill. Bill talked about his accomplishments in two ways. One was to document his many promotions with letters from his supervisors and later from the president of the company. Two, Bill had increased the efficiency of the accounting department through a complete computerization of its billing, inventory, and accounting process. Bill showed the interviewer several of the computerized programs that he had written. Bill then described how he could utilize an updated version of his project for the new employer's company. All he needed was the clearance and support from the company's officers. He was ready to go. He showed enthusiasm for his past accomplishments and projects. He gave the impression of high energy for any and all new projects and tasks. The employer was looking for an energetic, enthusiastic, and hardworking individual with the right skills. Bill demonstrated how he could meet these demands. He was, according to the employer, the right person for the job!

■ QUESTION 3

Another frequently asked question is **"What are your greatest strengths and your greatest weaknesses?"** Obviously, this is a double question. The employer will be looking for your ability to answer both parts of the question effectively. Your real weaknesses should not be stated as such. For example, if you have a problem showing up for work on time, then you do *not* want the employer to know this. You will handle this weakness on your own by developing the discipline necessary to be on time for work. The best advice is to take one of your strengths and make it a weakness. If you're an accountant, your weakness might be that you are "too precise and accurate and demand such work in others, but as a supervisor I am learning to be more tolerant of others and am able to help them." You will then correct the weakness by using words like "I am trying to improve; I am taking courses in that area." You correct your weakness. Maybe your lack of adequate computer skills is your greatest weakness for this particular job. You say, "My greatest weakness is my somewhat rusty computer skills, *but* I am registered to take an extensive computer course to improve my skills. In fact, I plan to continue taking computer courses to keep my skills on the cutting edge of technology." You corrected your deficiency. This strategy will work every time for you if you are well prepared. Most employers will recognize that everyone has weaknesses. The important issue for the employer is to hire someone who is striving to improve. Employers want to hire the best person for the job. If the employer thinks that you can learn the skill or improve through training, then he or she will hire you if this is only a minor weakness. Never say that you do not have any weaknesses. It will show that you have not thought enough about your abilities, skills, and work experience. Once again, the strategy is to take a strength and make it a weakness. Then you correct the weakness. The description below shows you this strategy through an actual case history.

> **REMEMBER to answer both parts of a *double question*.**

Joan, age 24, a new nursing graduate, was asked to describe her strengths and weaknesses. She responded by saying that her greatest strengths were her organizational abilities and her attention to detail. Her greatest weakness was that she became too emotionally attached to her patients; but the longer she worked as a nurse, the better she was able to handle her emotions because this was, in many situations, the best way to care for the patient. She was still empathetic and compassionate, but the care of the patient and supervision of the nursing team was her responsibility. She had the strength of character to carry out her responsibilities. From her portfolio, she showed the interviewer a letter from her clinical site ranking her as an outstanding nursing student with superior ability to act under pressure. The letter further stated that she had the qualities to be an excellent nurse and supervisor. Both her strengths and her weaknesses were taken from the Skill section of her S.T.A.R. Portfolio. She could document her greatest strength *and* her corrected weakness (which was really one of her strengths). In short, she was able to give the employer two strengths, or two very good reasons to hire her. She used her portfolio to answer his difficult double question.

■ QUESTION 4

The employer may ask you about your future career aspirations with a question such as **"What are your short- and long-term goals?"** The employer wants to know if you are motivated to working toward a higher academic degree or moving to a better position within the company. Here your S.T.A.R. Portfolio will be a help. You will say, "My short-term goal is to be an accounting clerk, and my long-term goal is to be an accountant with your company. I have just graduated with honors with my associate's degree in accounting." Here you produce your Honors Certificate from your Accomplishment section of your portfolio and also a letter of acceptance to a university or college, indicating that your long-term goal is to complete a four-year degree in accounting or business. "I have also been accepted to a transfer institution where I will start as a junior at ABC University. Here is my letter of acceptance. I am excited about my new job and the ways I can directly apply my education. It will help make my education more meaningful." Again, use your S.T.A.R. Portfolio's contents to successfully answer and document your statements.

■ QUESTION 5

Another question that the interviewer might use is **"Where do you see yourself heading in the next 5, 10, or 15 years?"** This question will tell the employer about your planning skills and about the amount of thought that went into your career plans. Again, be cautious about giving the impression that you will be leaving this company once you have additional experience or have completed your education. You will say that if hired, you plan to stay with the organization and that you look forward to advancement opportunities as you continue to learn though your work experience and increased education and knowledge of the business. From your S.T.A.R. Portfolio, you may want to use one of your letters of reference that states that you are a hard worker and that you learn quickly. The letter might also state that "ever since John started college, he always wanted to be a computer programmer. Even in high school, John was president of the computer club and excelled in mathematics. His long-term goal of becoming a systems analyst has always been in keeping with his career direction."

You might take out your letter of acceptance to a four-year college or university to indicate to the employer that you are serious about increasing your knowledge by completing your college degree at night. If you already have a B.S. or B.A. degree, you might show your graduate school acceptance letter or graduate transcript. Even if your knowledge is from non-credit courses, show your certificates and future plans to your prospective employer. These are part of your skill development, accomplishments, and training. These are your short- and long-term goals for the next 5, 10, or 15 years. They will be built into each section of your S.T.A.R. Portfolio. Anticipate and plan where you are headed in terms of your career and your personal growth by documenting your plan in terms of programs, certificates, or courses you might take.

One community college graduate who majored in liberal arts took from his portfolio an outline of his four-year business program, which he would be completing, and the individual courses he planned to take each semester to finish his degree. The employer was impressed by this person's ability to plan where he was headed in terms of not only the big picture, but in terms of specific details such as individual courses and the anticipated dates of completing each course. The employer needed employees who could put together a comprehensive plan for the future.

Now list under each of the four components in the S.T.A.R. Portfolio what your career plans will be for the next 5, 10, or 15 years. Use the S.T.A.R. Portfolio to accomplish this important planning stage. For example, under Skills, you might write those skills needed for your career goals in the next five years, such as public speaking, which you will be Trained for by attending Toastmasters, which will give you an Award and send you out to give speeches to local groups which you can use as a Reference.

Another Skill that you might want to develop is adequate state-of-the-art computer knowledge to manage your business more effectively. You plan to attend a local college for Training and apply it to your business, which would be an Accomplishment. Your business resources would be improved. Letters from your clients noting your improved services could be used as References.

Use the box below to fill in the planning stages for your S.T.A.R. Portfolio. Use pencil and be comprehensive and detailed. This plan may change in the next year or so, but for now you have a career plan to follow and guide your activities.

PLANNING STAGES IN THE S.T.A.R. PORTFOLIO

	5 YEARS	10 YEARS	15 YEARS
Career Goals			
Skills			
Training			
Accomplishments			
References
(These letters should reflect your abilities, goals, skills, training, and accomplishments)			

■ **QUESTION 6**

"Why did you choose this particular career area?" This question is a good one, and one you will shine on because you can use your S.T.A.R. Portfolio to help you. For example, if you were an accounting major, you might use the following scenario. From your S.T.A.R. Portfolio you take out your "Recognition for Honors Program in Mathematics." You then say that you have always been interested in the logical flow of numbers and patterns to find a solution to problems. Even in high school you always liked mathematics and went on to take a series of math courses in college which fit nicely into your accounting and computer science double major. You show the employer that you were thinking about using your math skills in a practical way. Thus, you have chosen two career areas that work closely together using your skills, that you enjoy, and that you are truly interested in pursuing as part of your career track. This answer tells the employer that you have the analytical skills to use your interests in a very practical way. It also indicates to the employer that you know what you want to do. This shows confidence, maturity, and a set of clearly stated objectives and abilities. The employer is looking for people who know their own goals and what type of positions they want. The employer will be impressed with your answer.

> **INCLUDE YOUR CAREER PLANS IN YOUR PORTFOLIO.**

Make a list of five reasons for choosing this particular career area, then mark each item as Skill, Training, Accomplishment, or Reference. If you like to work with people in a helping or caring profession, put that under Skills. If you like to work with your hands in making, building, or repairing things, put that under Skills. If you are pursuing a particular major, courses, or training, list these under Training in your portfolio. People choose careers because these career fields match with their own interest and personality types. You have Accomplishments and Awards and should list these no matter how irrelevant they may seem to you. They were part of your mini-decision to choose a particular career area. References are important because other people will be able to document your enthusiasm, interest, skills, abilities, potential, and accomplishments/goals. Make sure your references mention these in their letters of commendation and recommendation.

■ **QUESTION 7**

The employer will want to ask and know about your work experience and how you interacted with other people on the job. This question is a difficult one for the employer to evaluate even if you give a good answer. The employer will want to document your answer in terms of References and Recommendations. If the employer asks **"What did you like best and least about your current (or last) job?,"** the employer expects both parts of this double question to be answered. The employer is looking for such items as teamwork, experience, level of authority, management style, interaction with others, and how you solved conflicts or problems. Mention to the employer one or more of these in response to what you liked about the job. You will want to say what you liked and enjoyed best about your work. For example, Mary is an engineer at a large corporation. She wants to move to a medium-sized firm where she would feel a greater sense of belonging as a member of a team. She also wants to be able to work in a wider range of areas in terms of performing a variety of tasks. In her current position, she is limited to doing somewhat repetitive work without the feeling of accomplishing something new or challenging. So when the employer asked what she liked best, she was able to talk about her engineering skills, projects, and competencies. She added that she really liked the engineering area. What she did not like had to be couched into language that made her look good and that also made her current

> **S.T.A.R. PORTFOLIO**
> **MY CURRENT OR RECENT JOB**
>
> 1. What I liked most about my current position is . . .
>   Document (S.T.A.R.):
>
> 2. What I liked least about my current position is . . .
>   but your company will offer me the opportunity to . . .
>   Document (S.T.A.R.):

employer look good. She had to be tactful without whining or giving the impression that she would be difficult to work with as a member of a team. She answered this way. "I really enjoy what I do and the company I work for is really great, but I've been doing the same type of work so long that it is no longer a challenge. I'm looking for a job that will be challenging and will bring out all my skills and talents. I think that a company such as yours offers this opportunity." The employer may then ask, "What types of challenges or opportunities are you looking for?" Now is the time to exhibit your S.T.A.R. Portfolio. Some of your accomplishments in the engineering area that you truly enjoyed were recognized by others as exceptional. You would then say, "These are the types of projects I have done in the past and I think that I would have an opportunity to develop, expand, and complete this type of work with your company."

■ QUESTION 8

If you have just finished college or a vocational school, you might be asked a question about your education and specific course work. Again, your S.T.A.R. Portfolio will help you prepare for the interview and also help you answer the question. You will appear ready, poised, and organized. An open-ended approach would be a question such as **"Tell me about your educational background and training."** In answering this type of question, you want to mention your most recent educational experience. If you are in college, you would not mention your high school or grade school background. The only reason you might mention your high school background is to discuss any extraordinary activities, course work, or awards that would help you get the job. For example, if you were applying for a secretarial position and you had won an award for your outstanding typing speed or accuracy in high school, show the employer the award even though you are now in your second year of college. Remember, your S.T.A.R. Portfolio changes, grows, and develops just as you do. Have no fear in updating your portfolio.

Under Training in your S.T.A.R. Portfolio you will have all your degrees, transcripts, certificates, workshops, and seminars, so you can use the right ones to demonstrate your credentials and qualifications for the job. Use these items as tools to showcase your best qualities in order to sell yourself. Your accomplishments should also be introduced in response to a question about your background. "I was on the Dean's list for six semesters and graduated with high honors. Here is a copy of my National Dean's List Award." These accomplishments referring to your educational background will tell the employer that you are able to learn, that you are a hard worker and a completer, and that you must have been punctual with good attendance. These qualities are very much sought after by employers. Employers are looking for excellent employees who have the skills, training, and accomplishments to make their company grow and be economically successful in the world economy. In order to be competitive, viable, and dynamic, companies need people like you.

> **PRACTICE your interview answers OUT LOUD without the use of written materials.**

Take a practice run. If the employer wants to know about your educational background, write out your response and how you would use the educational sections of your S.T.A.R. Portfolio to demonstrate your background. Be specific and use complete sentences. Remember to say enough, but do not overdo it and become too verbose. Try the exercise on the following page to prepare yourself to answer this question. Practice saying your answers out loud without using a pat answer from your written responses. A brief outline will help you be concise, and appear knowledgeable and well spoken. Remember to phrase your responses in your own tone and language.

■ QUESTION 9

"Give me the three words that best describe you," asks an interviewer from a large Fortune 500 company. In answering this question, remember that the interviewer is looking for someone who knows what their Skills, Training, and Accomplishments are in terms of their personal qualities. A good answer is one that includes well-thought-out characteristics that can be documented from samples in your portfolio.

By using the S.T.A.R. Portfolio, you can not only answer this question clearly and quickly, you can in fact document your best qualities through specific examples. The answer to this question will plumb deeply into your personality and biographical information. Once again, the employer is searching your background for self-esteem, confidence, and the type of character you perceive yourself to have. Now list the three words that best describe you and the reasons why.

PRACTICE RESPONSE FOR INTERVIEW QUESTION 8

Let me tell you about my *educational background* in regards to my training, my accomplishments, and the skills I have developed to be successful in my organization:

■ **TRAINING:**

(Degrees) _____

(Courses) _____

(Seminars) _____

■ **AWARDS:**

_____

_____

_____

■ **ACCOMPLISHMENTS/PROJECTS:**

_____

_____

_____

■ **SKILLS:**

_____

_____

_____

_____

■ **REFERENCES:** *(Documenting skills, training, and accomplishments)*

_____

_____

_____

GIVE ME THREE WORDS OR DESCRIPTIONS THAT BEST DESCRIBE YOU

1. _____

Reasons why: _____

_____

_____

Documentation: _____

2. _____

Reasons why: _____

_____

_____

Documentation: _____

3. _____

Reasons why: _____

_____

_____

Documentation: _____

Having trouble getting started? Look at how others described you in letters from your portfolio. Choose the description for one quality that you can document from (1) Skills, (2) Training, and (3) Accomplishments, as Joan did. Joan is a 24-year-old who has just graduated from a community college with her A.S. Degree in Nursing, and has just passed her registered nurse examination. For her three descriptors she listed:

1. *Likeable:* She states that she is a team player who works well with all types of people. She truly wants to help patients get better and feel good. She documents this through the many thank-you notes and cards she has received on her student clinicals.

2. *Dedicated:* Joan is dedicated to the nursing field, taking courses to increase her knowledge and skills. She works hard and has completed extra training in Nursing for Senior Citizens and Advanced Practices in Clinical Care Nursing. Documents: Certifications in these areas.

3. *Persevering:* Joan completed her nursing degree, but it wasn't easy. She is a single parent who completed her G.E.D. (High School Equivalency) before entering a local community college. She started taking only two courses per semester until she had the time and, most of all, the confidence to continue her studies. She completed the Biology, Chemistry, Math, and Anatomy and Physiology courses she needed to apply for the program. After two years of preliminary courses, she was accepted into the professional nursing program. It didn't get any easier. She then had a full-time

clinical work site along with her other studies to contend with. She knew through discipline, excellent time management, and hard work that she would be successful, and she was. When she looks back on all her hard work she doesn't know how she did it. But she now plans to complete her B.S.N., her four-year Bachelor of Science Degree in Nursing, since her new job at the hospital will pay for her future education. She can be proud and can convey this sense of dedication and perseverance to her daughter. Joan is a survivor. She documents her perseverance by showing her degree and R.N. license.

In summary, use your S.T.A.R. Portfolio to answer this open-ended question. Always think in terms of documentation for your statements. Even if you have only a few items in your portfolio to support your claim, use them to the fullest. Brag a little about yourself, your skills, training, and accomplishments through your letters of recommendation. Be prepared and you will make difficult questions look easy to answer. It takes a lot of hard work and of course, perseverance. Keep at it and build your S.T.A.R. Portfolio to help you make your dreams come true.

■ QUESTION 10

The last question is **"Why should I hire you?"** This question can be asked in many different forms. The employer wants you to sum up the entire interview in order to see if you are the right person for the job. More than any others, the last words you utter to conclude your interview are going to be remembered. You may have hesitated or missed several earlier questions, but your summary is what the interviewer is going to base much of the final evaluation upon. You want to be prepared for this question. You can answer it beautifully with the help of your S.T.A.R. Portfolio. Here is how Bill Jones answered this question:

> **ENTHUSIASM AND A CLEAR SET OF GOALS** will shine through your S.T.A.R. Portfolio.

"I have the skills and training required for this job. They seem to match perfectly with the job as you described it. Also, I have worked successfully in this field for over three years. Just to repeat several of my major accomplishments . . . (describe setting up a new computerized accounting system for the company and streamlining the payroll department for over 70 employees, which gave your accounting department team more time to do detailed billing for customers). I am impressed with your company and your thoroughness. If I were offered the job, I would definitely take it. I appreciate your time and this opportunity. Do you need anything else from me, such as a transcript or references? . . . When do you think that I can expect to hear from you concerning this position?"

This answer summarizes for the interviewer the major reasons why you should be hired. You have the skills, training, experience, and accomplishments to do the job. You also demonstrated that you are well organized, likeable, a team player, and able to close the sale. You also told the interviewer that you are definitely interested in the job. The employer does not want to be rejected any more than you do. Your enthusiasm and clear goals will leave an excellent impression in the interviewer's mind. Now practice your answer in the box on the following page.

> **ON THE MOVE?**
> Keep your S.T.A.R. Portfolio updated and organized.

Write out your answer, and then practice reciting it out loud without your notes. Your remarks will then seem very natural, organized, and poised. You demonstrate once again to the employer why he or she should hire you. If you are prepared and confident, then you will have made an excellent impression on the interviewer and will have sold your most important product—*you*. You can be proud of a job well done. But do not stop here. Send a "thank you" letter with several of your reference letters included.

Keep working on getting the job until you have one. The job will usually be one that you are truly interested in taking and one that you will enjoy. Most people will work at 10 to 15 different jobs in their lifetime, changing careers 3 to 7 times. You can carry your transferable Skills, Training, Accomplishments, and References to your next job. In fact, your S.T.A.R. Portfolio will move with you throughout your working career. Keep it updated and be prepared for the next job or career opportunity that awaits you in the future. Keep a record of your accomplishments, awards, and current training. Everything is changing, growing, and evolving, including your career.

Let us review once again the 10 most frequently asked questions that employers ask job candidates and then have you practice your responses to 24 additional questions.

WHY SHOULD I HIRE YOU?

Write in complete sentences. Use a new sheet for each job for which you are applying.

You should hire me because I have the . . .

1. Skills

_____

_____

_____

2. Training

_____

_____

_____

3. Accomplishments/experience

_____

_____

_____

4. References

_____

_____

_____

5. Closing statement

_____

_____

_____

TEN QUESTIONS FREQUENTLY ASKED OF JOB APPLICANTS

1. Tell me about yourself and why you applied for this job.
2. Describe several of your main accomplishments. (Relate these to work and volunteer accomplishments.)
3. What are your greatest strengths and your greatest weaknesses?
4. What are your short-term and long range goals?
5. Where do you see yourself heading in the next 5, 10, or 15 years?
6. Why did you choose this particular career field?
7. What do you like best and what do you like least about your current job?
8. Tell me about your educational background and training.
9. Give me three words that best describe you. (This could be by you, a friend, an employee, or an employer.)
10. Why should I hire you?

24 PRACTICE QUESTIONS USING YOUR S.T.A.R. PORTFOLIO

1. If you were selecting a person for this type of job, what type of person would you hire?
2. Discuss your teamwork skills, using several examples as a team member or leader.
3. Describe a situation in which you handled stress on the job.
4. What are your problem-solving techniques regarding team members, a particular project, and a limited budget?
5. Why did you leave your previous position?
6. What motivates you to do your best work?
7. Discuss your management style.
8. Are you able to work as a team member or do you enjoy working alone?
9. How would you make suggestions for improvement to management? How would you think they would react?
10. Describe your ideal boss and the worst boss that you could have.
11. Describe your computer skills in regard to this particular job.
12. What kinds of people do you like and dislike working with?
13. How do you handle your emotions, such as anger, on the job? Describe several work or school situations that made you angry. How did you handle them?
14. How would your employees, teachers, employers, co-workers, or fellow students describe you?
15. You did well in school, but what makes you think you are qualified for this job?
16. Describe the most difficult decision you have had to make. How did you handle it?
17. What are your future plans for self-improvement, including education?
18. What has been your biggest mistake and how did you learn from it?
19. How do you deal with personality conflicts with co-workers? With bosses?
20. Tell me about your salary requirements.
21. How do you think that you can contribute to our business?
22. Describe your leadership positions at work, at school, or in a volunteer organization.
23. What would you do to be successful?
24. If you could start over again, what changes would you make in your life?

CONCLUSION

There are many ways to use your S.T.A.R. Portfolio as described in this chapter. Develop your own creative strategy to use. Your portfolio will be easy and fun to start. Keep developing it through your networking activities. Ask people for documentation if they say that you did a good job or made an excellent presentation. All these documents will be listed in your master S.T.A.R. Portfolio. When a specific job arises, you will be ready to select documentation to be used in your cover letter, phone conversations, and obviously at the job interview itself . . . Your quest will continue until you get the job of your dreams. Creating, updating, and using your S.T.A.R. Portfolio puts you on a straight and clear pathway to achieving your goals. Once you know where you are headed, it is easier to get there— with the help, of course, of your S.T.A.R. Portfolio.

> **REMEMBER** to identify the reason why the question is being asked.

58 Examples of Tables of Contents for Your S.T.A.R. Portfolio

4

Your S.T.A.R. Portfolio Table of Contents serves as an outline for your portfolio and accompanies your cover letter and resume. Make the outline descriptive and eye-catching. Tweak the interest of a prospective employer and support your claims of skills, training, accomplishments, and references.

Before creating a resume and supporting portfolio, establish clear objectives. These are generally stated in functional terms such as (1) to develop new markets through research, analysis, and promotion; (2) to build teams through establishing rapport, determining needs, and communicating goals; and (3) to design an improved "widget" through revision of specifications, computer-assisted design, and field testing. Espouse your objectives with supporting examples of skills. Demonstrate a minimum of three skills. You may choose to demonstrate as many as eight skills. Although you generally concentrate upon three to five primary skills in communicating with a prospective employer, you can use other skills to demonstrate "value added" capabilities that you bring to the position. You do not need to use each of your entries with every portfolio presentation. The broader your selection of entries, the greater the ability you have to customize your portfolio for each employment opportunity.

Skills are best derived from training or work projects. Rummage through your work or training projects. Find samples that support your objective. Where you are unable to locate existing samples, create facsimiles. In S.T.A.R. Portfolio #7, Biological Science/Chemical Laboratory Science, this histologist demonstrated her skill in written communication by producing laboratory reports she had previously filed. In S.T.A.R. Portfolio #54, this recent Office Administrative Support graduate demonstrated word-processing skills through a course prerequisite typing test. In S.T.A.R. Portfolio #15, Chemistry Laboratory Supervisor, this portfolio developer needed to write an after-the-fact description of committee participation to demonstrate teamwork skills.

Training is best demonstrated by originals or copies of earned degrees, professional licenses, and certifications. The Training section of S.T.A.R. Portfolio #45, Operations/Training Management, reflects the owner's training aimed at skill improvement and confirmed through certificates and a letter of completion.

Presentation of quality accomplishments sets you apart from the crowd. Originality is merited here. Completed projects, awards, recognition, inventions, publications, finished projects, and statistics are good demonstrations of accomplishments.

Note that the S.T.A.R. Portfolio sample #18, Construction/Facilities Management, under accomplishments #4 states "photographs of renovated properties including the Baskervilles Estate, the property immortalized in Sir Arthur Conan Doyle's Hound of the Baskervilles." By alluding to a famous edifice on which he worked, this job seeker strikes a note of interest that might gain him an interview by a curious employer who appreciates literature, history, or both. This inclusion also supports his claim to expertise in historical preservation construction.

The most common form of reference is the letter. The most common sources of letters of reference are current and past supervisors, faculty, and colleagues. Letters of reference should reflect and support your skills and accomplishments. The best way to ensure this is to outline the contents requested or write the letter yourself and submit it for signature. Secure and include in this section any favorably stated letter. The best letters are current, speak favorably about you, and are well written by someone of stature.

Review the following S.T.A.R. Portfolio Contents before completing your own. For purposes of space we have used a narrow column for our sample tables of contents. You will probably wish to use the full page width for your own table of contents.

S.T.A.R. PORTFOLIOS THAT YOU CAN USE

PORTFOLIO	COLLEGE MAJOR	OBJECTIVE
1	Accounting	Accounting
2	Accounting	Golf Club Management
3	Accounting/Medical Insurance	Medical Insurance Manager
4	Airline Reservation Certificate	Customer Service Agent (Airline)
5	Applied Computer Technology/History	Operations Supervisor
6	Auto Body Management	Claims Estimator
7	Biological Science/Clinical Laboratory Sciences	Laboratory Technology/Histology
8	Biology/Pharmacy	Pharmacy Administration
9	Business	Bookkeeper/Accountant
10	Business Administration	Account Executive
11	Business Administration	Production Planning/Supervision
12	Business Administration	Sales/Marketing
13	Business Administration	Underwriter/Lender
14	Business/Computer Science	Computer Science
15	Chemistry	Chemistry Laboratory Supervisor
16	Communications	Journalism
17	Communications/Marketing	PR/Marketing
18	Construction Experience/Journeyman	Construction/Facilities Management
19	Computer Science	Instructor
20	Counseling/Higher Education	Student Services/Administration
21	Criminology/Sociology	Counselor, Juvenile Offenders/Juvenile Probation
22	Dietetics	Dietitian/Nutritionist

(continued)

PORTFOLIO	COLLEGE MAJOR	OBJECTIVE
23	Economics/MBA/Finance	Financial Management
24	Electrical Engineering	Quality Engineering/Technical Support
25	Electronics	Technical Support/Repair
26	Elementary Education	Elementary Teaching
27	Engineering	Design Engineer
28	English	District/Regional Sales Manager
29	English Education	Teaching/Advising
30	Environmental Science and Management	Environmental Science and Safety Manager
31	Geology	Environmental Engineering
32	History	Project/Support Management
33	Hotel/Hospitality Management	Hotel/Restaurant Manager
34	Housekeeping Supervision Experience	Housekeeping Supervision
35	Industrial Arts	Maintenance Operations Management
36	Journalism	Public Relations for the Arts
37	Labor Relations	Human Resources/Labor Relations Management
38	Legal Secretarial Specialist	Legal Secretary/Paralegal
39	Management	Sales/Customer Service
40	Mathematics	Service/Operational Projects Management
41	Mechanical Drafting and Design Technology	Drafting/Design
42	Mechanical Engineering	Mechanical Engineer
43	Nursing	Nursing
44	Occupational Therapy Assistant	C.O.T.A.
45	Operations Experience	Operations/Training Management
46	Pharmacy	Pharmacist
47	Physical Therapist	Physical Therapist
48	Psychology	Chemical Dependency Counselor
49	Psychology	Fundraiser
50	Psychology/Education	Social Worker
51	Quantitative Business Analysis/MBA	Analysis/Financial Management
52	Retail Management	Buyer/Retail Merchandising
53	Secondary Education	Investigation/Loss Prevention
54	Secretarial Science	Office Administrative Support
55	Speech Pathology	Speech Pathologist/Audiologist
56	Teacher Education	Teaching
57	Technical Communications	Technical Writer
58	Visual Communications	Visual Artist/Designer/Illustrator

Here is a suggested format for your S. T. A. R. table of contents. It is the one we've used for the following examples.

STAR PORTFOLIO CONTENTS

COLLEGE MAJOR:

OBJECTIVE:

■ SKILLS

1.

2.

3.

4.

5.

■ TRAINING

1.

2.

3.

4.

5.

■ ACCOMPLISHMENTS

1.

2.

3.

4.

5.

■ REFERENCES

1.

2.

3.

4.

5.

STAR PORTFOLIO CONTENTS 1

COLLEGE MAJOR: **Accounting**
OBJECTIVE: **Accounting**

■ SKILLS

1. Special recognition, Sales (Second in the region for sales of house siding)
2. Article from school newspaper (Recognized as team leader for peer tutoring)
3. Thank-you note (Tax consultant for elderly, tax laws, procedures)
4. Computer skills (Sample reports and programs)

■ TRAINING

1. Diplomas (A.S. and B.S. in Accounting from CCAC and Penn State)
2. Certificate in Taxation (H&R Block)
3. Certificate of Workshop Completion (Accounting Applications in Windows)
4. Dale Carnegie (Certificate)

■ ACCOMPLISHMENTS

1. Awards (Dean's list, Outstanding Student of the Year)
2. Co-op evaluations (Two year co-op assignment in tax accounting)
3. Tax return (Produced on computer program designed by applicant)
4. Sample (Small business accounting records)
5. Published article ("Savings for Small Business Owners Through Computerized Accounting")

■ REFERENCES

1. Letter of Commendation (H&R Block supervisor)
2. Letter of Reference (Private tax client)
3. Letter of Reference (Co-op placement supervisor emphasizing performance and attendance)

STAR PORTFOLIO CONTENTS 2

COLLEGE MAJOR: **Accounting**
OBJECTIVE: **Golf Club Management**

■ SKILLS

1. Coordinating special events (List of club events, photos, newsletters)
2. Conducting tournaments (List tournaments, photos, letters)
3. Teaching golf lessons (Letters of praise from clients)
4. Managing golf shop (Policy and procedure manual)

■ TRAINING

1. B.A. in Accounting (Degree)
2. A.S. in Accounting with Honors (Degree)
3. Sales Certificate (Certificate)

■ ACCOMPLISHMENTS

1. Increased female membership (Women's Golf Association dates and events)
2. Election to PGA membership (Attached)
3. All-States Individual Tournament (2nd Place)
4. Committee memberships (Golf, Greens, and Safety committees)

■ REFERENCES

1. Letter of Reference from golf pro listing supervision and management
2. Letter of Supervision documenting sales capabilities
3. Letter of Appreciation from club members and clinic students
4. Letter of Recommendation from previous supervisor from golf club documenting work with club members

STAR PORTFOLIO CONTENTS 3

COLLEGE MAJOR: **Accounting/Medical Insurance**

OBJECTIVE: **Medical Insurance Manager**

■ SKILLS

1. Proficient with computer applications (List software knowledge and sample databases)
2. Knowledge of medical insurance codes (ICD-9 training)
3. Communication skills (Able to articulate insurance options/policies in a professional and comprehensible manner)
4. Organizational skills (Detail-oriented)

■ TRAINING

1. A.S. in Accounting (Degree)
2. Certified Medical Insurance Specialist (Certificate with highest honors)
3. B.S. Degree (Transcript)
4. Health Professional Management Course (Certificate)

■ ACCOMPLISHMENTS

1. Dean's list (Letter of Acknowledgment)
2. Member of Pittsburgh Health Professionals Association (Certificate)
3. Perfect attendance (Certificate)
4. Phi Theta Kappa (Membership certificate)

■ REFERENCES

1. Letter of Reference from instructor (Noting dedication as a student)
2. Letter of Reference from former employer (Detailing proficiency of work as office manager)
3. Letter of Thanks from church official (Duties as a layperson within the church)
4. Letter of Recommendation from work supervisor (Emphasizing insurance and organizational skills)

STAR PORTFOLIO CONTENTS 4

COLLEGE MAJOR: **Airline Reservation Certificate**

OBJECTIVE: **Customer Service Agent (Airline)**

■ SKILLS

1. Data entry/Computer skills (Samples of data entry)
2. Interpersonal Relations (Phone training certification)
3. Knowledge of FAA regulations (Passed test)
4. Weight and Balance for A/C (Passed test)

■ TRAINING

1. In-house training including ticketing, domestic/international baggage agreements, cargo, package procedures, and weight and balance. (Certificate in Travel)
2. CPR certification (Current certificate)

■ ACCOMPLISHMENTS

1. Commendation Letters from customers (Letters)
2. Perfect attendance award (Award)
3. Free upgrade passes for attendance (Reward certification)
4. Acknowledgment from supervisors of a good job performance (Letters from supervisors)

■ REFERENCES

1. Station Manager, PIT/Dayton, documenting attendance and performance
2. Administration Manager, Philadelphia, documenting people skills
3. Station Manager, Dayton, documenting team skills, learning ability
4. Personnel Supervisor, Philadelphia, documenting attendance and excellent phone skills

STAR PORTFOLIO CONTENTS 5

COLLEGE MAJOR: **Applied Computer Technology/History**

OBJECTIVE: **Operations Specialist**

■ SKILLS

1. Planning (List of planning accomplishments, photos, drawings)
2. Organizing (Interoffice memos on project development)
3. Identifying and implementing solutions (Projects implemented)
4. Cost Savings (3 years of budgets with reduced operating costs)

■ TRAINING

1. A.S. in Applied Computer Technology (Degree with highest honors)
2. B.S. in History (Degree with highest honors)
3. Productivity Through Quality (Certificate)
4. Total Quality Management Training (Advanced certificate)

■ ACCOMPLISHMENTS

1. Organized repairs with current employees, saving 65% outsourcing (Repair estimates vs. actual cost)
2. Converted from manual to automated supply and distribution system (Transfer letter of employee maintaining manual system)
3. Oversaw installation of office computerization (User manual training schedule)
4. Redesigned work flow for production, saving $45,000 (Schedules and reassignments)

■ REFERENCES

1. Computer Science faculty member (Letter of Reference relating computer skills)
2. Planning director (Letter of Reference denoting planning accomplishments)
3. Vice president (Letter of Commendation recognizing "Outstanding Employee")
4. TQM trainer (Letter of Commendation acknowledging leadership ability)

STAR PORTFOLIO CONTENTS 6

COLLEGE MAJOR: **Auto Body Management**

OBJECTIVE: **Claims Estimator**

■ SKILLS

1. Mechanical repair (Mechanic certificate from high school, listing knowledge of diagnostics)
2. Computer knowledge (Sample from an estimator's program)
3. Auto body repair (Photos of jobs completed)
4. Valid driver's license/good driving record (Proof of insurance and photo license ID)

■ TRAINING

1. Business Management (Degree, technical college)
2. Vocational schooling (Auto Body diploma)
3. Estimator's license (License)

■ ACCOMPLISHMENTS

1. Graduated on Dean's List (Dean's list certificate)
2. I-Car Collision Repair 2000 Certificate (Certificate)
3. Graduated from vocational school with high honors (Certificate)
4. Rebuilt 15 cars for hobby (Pictures and list of car models)

■ REFERENCES

1. Letter of Reference from a business management faculty member
2. Letter of Reference from auto body instructor
3. Letter of Reference from body shop owner
4. Letter of Commendation from insurance company

STAR PORTFOLIO CONTENTS 7

COLLEGE MAJOR: **Biological Science/Clinical Laboratory Sciences**

OBJECTIVE: **Laboratory Technology/Histology**

■ SKILLS

1. Organization and attention to detail (recordkeeping, lab reports)
2. Basic lab skills (demonstrated ability—supervisor evaluation)
3. Written communication skills for reporting (examples of reports)
4. OSHA standards knowledge (accreditation, certification)
5. Oral communication skills (evaluation from supervisor)

■ TRAINING

1. B.S. Biological Sciences/Clinical Laboratory Science (Degree)
2. Member ACPA/Certified Histologist (Membership)
3. First Aid/CPR/Medical Facility in Safety (Certificate of Training)
4. Graduate, specialized advanced training (Transcripts)

■ ACCOMPLISHMENTS

1. Trained staff members (Student and supervisor evaluations)
2. Member of Safety Committee—Secretary (Explanation of duties and accomplishments)
3. Developed immunohistological technique (Report of findings)
4. Emergency HAZMAT cleanup personnel (Procedural manual)
5. Scholarship/funding for further research (Grant proposal)

■ REFERENCES

1. Letter of Reference from immediate supervisor (Excellent quality of work)
2. Letter of Reference from chairman of Biological Sciences Department (Strong academic performance)
3. Letter of Reference, personal recommendation (High moral character, responsible)
4. Letter of Reference from Safety Commission president (Dedication and abilities)

STAR PORTFOLIO CONTENTS 8

COLLEGE MAJOR: **Biology/Pharmacy**

OBJECTIVE: **Pharmacy Administration**

■ SKILLS

1. Supervision (List and job descriptions of supervisory works, letter from university supervisor of training pharmacy interns)
2. Customer service (Year-end audit showing zero accidents in treatment preparations)
3. Crisis management (Written evaluation of aminoglycoside levels with recommended drug therapies avoiding medical crisis)
4. Inventory control (Citations of 5 consecutive years rated as "top shop" in the chain for maintenance of narcotics inventory)

■ TRAINING

1. B.S. in Pharmacy with honors (Degree)
2. B.S. in Biology (Degree)
3. Continuing Education: pharmacy seminars (Certificate)
4. State Pharmacy License (License)

■ ACCOMPLISHMENTS

1. Printout of database of computerized mail order customers vs. photocopy of ledger accounting of customers
2. Written recognition of preparation of 160 chemotherapy treatments over 4-year period with zero errors.
3. 100% accuracy rate in narcotics inventory at 3 hospitals (Annual audit reports)
4. Oriented/trained physicians and patients (Workshop evaluations, thank-you letters)

■ REFERENCES

1. Hospital C.E.O. (Letter of Reference recognizing outstanding service)
2. District supervisor (Letter of Reference describing management abilities)
3. Head nurse (Letter of Commendation for quick intervention in preparation of alternative pharmacological therapies)
4. Pharmacy supervisor (Letter of Reference documenting accuracy)

STAR PORTFOLIO CONTENTS 9

COLLEGE MAJOR: **Business**

OBJECTIVE: **Bookkeeper/Accountant**

■ SKILLS

1. Bookkeeping (Sample accounts payable and receivable records)
2. Payroll (Sample payroll)
3. Training (Programs, booklets developed for training new employees)
4. Computers (Sample software for accounting)

■ TRAINING

1. A.S. Degree in Business with high honors (Degree)
2. Accounting Certificate (Certificate)
3. Computer courses (Transcript)
4. Benefits seminars (Certificates and Programs)

■ ACCOMPLISHMENTS

1. Trained and supervised over 30 employees (List types and productivity levels)
2. Employee of the Month (Award)
3. Installed new computerized accounting system (Article)
4. Implemented benefits program (Significant savings for company with statistics, Letter of Recognition from board of directors)

■ REFERENCES

1. Letter of Reference from supervisor (Saved company significant costs)
2. Letter of Reference from previous accounting supervisor (Excellent worker)
3. Letter of Reference from accounting faculty (Accounting skills)
4. Letter of Reference from computer faculty member (Computer skills)

STAR PORTFOLIO CONTENTS 10

COLLEGE MAJOR: **Business Administration**

OBJECTIVE: **Account Executive**

■ SKILLS

1. Marketing (Example of strategic plans, records of growth and production)
2. Public relations (Audience and supervisor evaluation; public opinion survey; press releases and reports)
3. Accounting (Bookkeeping records, monthly and year-end reports)
4. Finance (Records and reports)
5. Computer skills (List of courses taken, programs, proficient usage)

■ TRAINING

1. G.I.A. diamond grading courses (Certificate)
2. Excel Computer Training (Documentation)
3. Sales seminars (Documentation, presentation materials)
4. Graduate-level courses (transcripts, syllabi)

■ ACCOMPLISHMENTS

1. Vice-President of Outing Club (Duties performed)
2. Increased sales by double-digit percent every year (Year-end reports)
3. Student supervision of college dining hall (Job description, supervisor evaluation of management abilities)
4. Lab leader of ceramic lab (Roles and responsibilities, evaluation)
5. Council of trustees at church (Financial decision-making body of the church; summary of issues)

■ REFERENCES

1. Professor of Marketing (Excellent skill level and performance)
2. Supervisor of all dining halls (Excellent manager and group relationships)
3. Letter of Reference from summer job supervisors (Responsible and dedicated)
4. Letter of Personal Recommendation from fellow trustee (Dependable, highly concerned, involved)

STAR PORTFOLIO CONTENTS 11

COLLEGE MAJOR: **Business Administration**
OBJECTIVE: **Production-Planning Supervision**

■ SKILLS

1. Planning (Marketing strategy plan, including cost sheet reflecting annual cost savings in labor and materials)

2. Scheduling (Daily schedules with specific work assignments)

3. Inventory control (Computerized printout of cost/materials supplies for new manufacturing company)

4. Supervision (Factory layout and work processing system plan, including flow charts showing line of command and positions reporting to supervisors)

■ TRAINING

1. B.S. in Business Administration (Degree)

2. Development Dimensions International Customer Service Seminar (Certificate)

3. American Management Association Production Supervision (Certificate)

4. Graphic Arts Technical Foundation Estimating Course (Certificate)

■ ACCOMPLISHMENTS

1. Successful proprietorship (Schedule C of IRS 1040)

2. Cost savings (Invoices)

3. Increased production (Year-end reports)

4. Planning project (Factory layout design)

■ REFERENCES

1. Chief financial officer (Letter of Reference attributing maintenance of profit margins to production planning and implementation)

2. Plant manager (Letter of Reference noting efficiency and cost savings)

3. Employee (Letter of Reference describing employee and customer relations)

4. Company president (Thank-you memo for extra effort in getting new facility up and running on time)

STAR PORTFOLIO CONTENTS 12

COLLEGE MAJOR: **Business Administration**
OBJECTIVE: **Sales/Marketing**

■ SKILLS

1. Seasoned sales professional (9 years of sales records)

2. Ability to maintain long-term buying relationship (5-year report on sales volume to existing customers, letters of appreciation from customers)

3. Strong analytical skills (Wrote reports of new products introduced based on research of demographic analysis; samples attached)

4. Strong planning skills (Sample of sales promotions and strategic plan for marketing for past and next three years)

■ TRAINING

1. B.S. in Business Administration (Degree)

2. Influencing at the Buyer's Desk (Warner-Lambert Training Seminar)

3. Negotiating the Deal (Warner-Lambert Training Seminar)

4. Tele-Magic (Observer Publishing Training Seminar)

■ ACCOMPLISHMENTS

1. 1997 Mid-Atlantic Representative of the Year (Award)

2. 1995 District Representative of the Year (Award)

3. 1996 Manufacturer of the Year (Award from Wholesalers Association)

4. Consistent achievement of sales goals (Annual sales reports)

■ REFERENCES

1. Professors' Letters of Reference (Noting marketing strategies & management)

2. Past supervisors (Three letters documenting sales ability)

3. Account buyers (Letters of Commendations on service)

4. Personal (Letters of Personal Recommendation documenting personality, persistence, enthusiasm, and leadership)

STAR PORTFOLIO CONTENTS 13

COLLEGE MAJOR: **Business Administration**
OBJECTIVE: **Underwriter/Lender**

■ SKILLS

1. Computer skills (PC) (Spreadsheets of loans, sample database, management of clients)
2. Consumer Lending Guidelines knowledge (Test score)
3. Rapport building with internal and external customers (Customer satisfaction surveys)
4. Management skills (Supervise 6 people; statement of management philosophy & vision statement)

■ TRAINING

1. B.S. in Business Administration (Degree)
2. Residential Lending classes (Certificate)
3. Systems Programming Instruction (Certificate and Course Contents)
4. Sales Workshop classes (Bank Certificate)

■ ACCOMPLISHMENTS

1. Promoted from processor to underwriter (Letter of Congratulations)
2. Promoted from Underwriter to credit manager (Letter of Acceptance)
3. Highest Sales Award for Department (Award)
4. Nominated Most Valuable Asset to Credit Department (In-house publication)

■ REFERENCES

1. Systems analyst at large bank, Letter of Reference (Troubleshooting)
2. Vice president of Retail Credit and Student Loans (Bank)
3. Retail asset manager (Bank)
4. Credit manager and customer lending supervisor (Bank)

STAR PORTFOLIO CONTENTS 14

COLLEGE MAJOR: **Business/Computer Science**
OBJECTIVE: **Computer Science**

■ SKILLS

1. Web Page Design (Samples in HTML, Java Script, Page Maker)
2. Writer (Newspaper articles authored)
3. Photographer (Samples in computerized book for marketing, postcards, fliers)
4. Graphic Layouts (Samples of paper advertisements, mailers, titling)
5. Computer Projects (List of software and sample computer projects)

■ TRAINING

1. A.S. in Computer Science with high honors (Degree and transcript)
2. A.S. in Business Management with high honors (Degree and transcript)
3. American Sign Language (Certificate)
4. German (Correspondence in German to company in Europe)

■ ACCOMPLISHMENTS

1. FCC Amateur License (Attached)
2. Member of Pittsburgh Film Workers Association (Certificate)
3. C++ and Java projects (Attached)
4. Phi Theta Kappa honorary fraternity (Membership certificate)
5. Member of Linda Speigal Design Group (List of projects)

■ REFERENCES

1. Computer Science Faculty Letter of Reference concerning computer skills
2. Computer Science Faculty Letter of Reference concerning skills
3. Letter of Reference from newspaper supervisor (Emphasizing writing/photography skills)
4. Letter of Reference from work supervisor (Emphasizing marketing and advertising skills)

STAR PORTFOLIO CONTENTS 15

COLLEGE MAJOR: **Chemistry**

OBJECTIVE: **Chemistry Laboratory Supervisor**

■ **SKILLS**

1. Production (Description of revised production system)
2. Analysis (Client laboratory report)
3. Teamwork (Description of committee participation)
4. Quality control (Reports)

■ **TRAINING**

1. B.S. in Chemistry with honors (Degree)
2. Seminar in Organic Chemistry (Certificate)
3. Noncredit computer courses in keyboarding, databases, and spreadsheets (Certificates)

■ **ACCOMPLISHMENTS**

1. Research summary of improved titration method
2. Reduction of precious metal waste (Assay report)
3. Laboratory notes demonstrating 15% increase in accuracy
4. ISO 9000 quality control certification (Letter of Verification)

■ **REFERENCES**

1. Department supervisor (Letter of Reference evaluating competency in organic chemistry)
2. Plant supervisor (Letter of Reference commending production coordination)
3. Human resources director (Letter of thanks for valuable service as member of search committee)

STAR PORTFOLIO CONTENTS 16

COLLEGE MAJOR: **Communications**

OBJECTIVE: **Journalism**

■ **SKILLS**

1. Good writing skills (Sample articles)
2. Good observer/researcher (Sample of publications)
3. Computer use/technology (example of uses)
4. Organizational skills (Supervisor evaluation, description of evaluation of personal record system)
5. Grammar and editing (copies of written materials in various draft stages)

■ **TRAINING**

1. B.A. in Communications (Degree)
2. Internship at local newspaper (Sample work)
3. Journalism mentor (Letter of Recommendation regarding growth and progress)
4. Training in layout and design (Sample work)

■ **ACCOMPLISHMENTS**

1. Outstanding Student Journalist of the Year (Award)
2. Editor of campus newspapers (Copies of several editions)
3. National Association of Journalists (Membership)
4. Article chosen for national publication (Copy of article)
5. Winner of essay contest/scholarship (Copy of essay)

■ **REFERENCES**

1. Letter of Reference from college faculty (Writing ability)
2. Letter of Reference from intern supervisor (Good evaluation)
3. Letter of Personal Recommendation from mentor (Personal and professional growth)
4. Letters of Reference from supervisors of campus newspaper (Excellent quality of work)

STAR PORTFOLIO CONTENTS 17

COLLEGE MAJOR: **Communications/Marketing**
OBJECTIVE: **PR/Marketing**

■ SKILLS

1. Sales (Recruiter's evaluation from supervisor, letters from clients praising company, $360,000 sales first year)
2. Writing/editing (Sample business plan, master's thesis included, sample weekly newsletter)
3. Graphic design (Sample brochures, menus, business cards)
4. Accounting Certificate in accounting, H&R Block (Certificate)
5. Supervision (Supervised 16 stewards for U.E. Supervisor's annual evaluation)
6. Marketing Supervisor for telemarketing (Sample mail pieces and published newsletter for union)

■ TRAINING

1. A.S. in Accounting/Finance (Degree)
2. B.A. in Communications (Degree)
3. M.A. Corporate Communications and Marketing (Degree)
4. PA Real Estate License (Residential and Commercial) (4 Courses)

■ ACCOMPLISHMENTS

1. Phi Theta Kappa (Distinguish Scholar Award, Essay Award)
2. Graduated with high honors (Certificate)
3. Wall Street Junior Achievement Award, Academic Excellence in College (Award)
4. Staff writer, Dialogue, department of communications (Monthly magazine sample)
5. Vice president, student government and Phi Theta Kappa (Membership, Letters, Programs)

■ REFERENCES

1. Journalism professor's Letter of Reference regarding writing skills
2. Graduate professor's Letter of Commendation regarding thesis
3. Real estate broker's Letter of Reference on job performance
4. Accounting supervisor's Letter of Reference regarding accounting on tax work

STAR PORTFOLIO CONTENTS 18

COLLEGE MAJOR: **Construction Experience/ Journeyman**
OBJECTIVE: **Construction-Facilities Management**

■ SKILLS

1. Historical preservation (Newspaper feature article)
2. Design (Drawing samples, photographs of projects)
3. Project management (Photographs at various stages, invoices for building supplies)
4. Liaison with local authorities (Construction permits authorizing and describing nature of work to be done)

■ TRAINING

1. Carpentry (Certificate)
2. Building Materials (Certificate)
3. Construction Safety (Certificate)
4. Building Code Regulations (Certificate)

■ ACCOMPLISHMENTS

1. Developed customer loyalty (Company correspondence demonstrating client contentment and commitment to company)
2. Increased company profits (Contracts for work projects acquired)
3. Acquired new clients (List of projects and revenues generated)
4. Renovation of historic properties (Photographs of renovated properties including the Baskerville Estate, the property immortalized in Sir Arthur Conan Doyle's *Hounds of the Baskerville)*

■ REFERENCES

1. Letter of Reference (Former employer describing skills and accomplishments displayed in prior position)
2. Letter of Thanks (Former client stating satisfaction with the completed project and quality of process)
3. Letter of Commendation (Former vendor remarking on the "highest levels of professional deportment")

STAR PORTFOLIO CONTENTS 19

COLLEGE MAJOR: **Computer Science**
OBJECTIVE: **Instructor**

■ SKILLS

1. Computer skills/projects (Samples of software and projects)
2. Technical writer (Articles written and technical manuals created)
3. Communication (Samples of written documents)
4. Instructor (Samples of syllabus, course outline, books written for class)
5. Training (Training of new employees, students, sample manuals)

■ TRAINING

1. A.S. in Computer Science with high honors (Degree and transcript)
2. B.S. in Education with honors (Degree and transcript)
3. United States Air Force (Training certificates)
4. Seminars (Certificates)

■ ACCOMPLISHMENTS

1. Accolades from military for serving during time of war (Medals)
2. Development of courses (Sample chapter)
3. Certified Microsoft Consultant (Certificate)
4. Upper level instructor at technical college
5. Teaching Award from college (Certificate)

■ REFERENCES

1. Letter of Reference (Noting communication and computer skills)
2. Letters of Commendation (Thank-you letters from former students)
3. Letter of Recommendation (Emphasizing technical knowledge and teaching skills)
4. Letter of Recommendation (Emphasizing leadership and personality)

STAR PORTFOLIO CONTENTS 20

COLLEGE MAJOR: **Counseling/Higher Education**
OBJECTIVE: **Student Services/Administration**

■ SKILLS

1. Counseling (Thank-you letters from clients, supervisor's evaluation)
2. Grant writing (List of grants totaling over $800,000, sample grant)
3. Supervision (List of counseling staff, functions, and programs)
4. Computer applications (Sample Web page, computerized job match system for four campuses)
5. Administration (Description of student award programs, newspaper articles describing job shadowing programs and collaborative work with employers, CLEP testing, schools, and community agencies)

■ TRAINING

1. B.A.s in Psychology, Philosophy (Degrees)
2. M.Ed., Ph.D. Counseling Psychology (Degrees)
3. National Board for Certified Counselors (Certificate)
4. PA State Psychologist License (License)

■ ACCOMPLISHMENTS

1. Publications (List of books and publications, book covers included)
2. Teaching (Student evaluations of courses, list of courses taught)
3. Grant awards (Certificate of Recognition from college president)
4. Projects (Career Week, COOP, CLEP, internship, DWEPT fliers and articles)
5. Professional conference coordination and workshops (Brochures attached)
6. Board of Directors (List of boards served on, Letters from board)

■ REFERENCES

1. Dean of Students, immediate college supervisor (Contributions to institution)
2. Vice President of Academic and Student Services (Outstanding leadership)
3. Executive Director, Chamber of Commerce (Collaborative efforts)
4. Assistant Dean of Social Work (Letter of Reference on teamwork, partnerships)
5. Grant project director (Letter of Commendation)

STAR PORTFOLIO CONTENTS 21

COLLEGE MAJOR: **Criminology/Sociology**

OBJECTIVE: **Counselor, Juvenile Offenders/ Juvenile Probation**

■ **SKILLS**

1. Good communication skills (Sample reports, presentation materials)
2. Ability to understand another's perspective (Work evaluations, participant evaluations)
3. Strong work ethic (Supervisor evaluation)
4. Compassion/understanding (Supervisor and client evaluations)
5. Public speaking (Training and workshops)

■ **TRAINING**

1. B.S. in Criminology (Degree)
2. Minor in Sociology
3. Workshops/specialized training on drug/alcohol abuse (Certificate)
4. Internship at juvenile detention center (Supervisor evaluation)

■ **ACCOMPLISHMENTS**

1. Criminology Association (Membership)
2. Peer Advisor for orientation (Work with incoming freshmen, list of programs/activities participated in)
3. Resident Assistant (List of programs implemented, supervisor evaluation)
4. Research on teens and alcohol abuse (Copy of study and findings)
5. Dean's list (Record of academic achievements)

■ **REFERENCES**

1. Letter of Reference from faculty regarding class achievement
2. Letter of Reference from supervisor (Work performance)
3. Letter of Reference from internship supervisor (Work performance, growth, ability to get along with others, skills with clients)
4. Letter of Reference from coordinator of peer advisor programs (Evaluation of ability to work well with others, creativity)

STAR PORTFOLIO CONTENTS 22

COLLEGE MAJOR: **Dietetics**

OBJECTIVE: **Dietitian/Nutritionist**

■ **SKILLS**

1. Educating the public (Weekly column in local paper)
2. Screening clients' habits (Surveys of eating habits and graphs of patterns though food groups)
3. Planning diets (Sample diets coordinating proper nutrition through food groups)
4. Medical nutrition therapy (Sample diets for specific illnesses)
5. Implementing latest food and nutrition research (Sample dietary plans for use with 5 different age groups)

■ **TRAINING**

1. B.S. in Dietetics (Degree)
2. M.S. in Nutrition (Degree)
3. State License (License)
4. Registered Dietitian (R.D. credentials)

■ **ACCOMPLISHMENTS**

1. Head dietitian in large nursing home (Letter from director, job description, programs)
2. Consultant (List of clients, including hospitals & home health care agencies)
3. Creative marketing strategies (Sample advertisements)
4. Nutritional Awareness Award (Award)
5. Special recipes developed for American Heart association (Recipes, published in AHA recipe book)

■ **REFERENCES**

1. Letter of Reference from nursing home administrator documenting services
2. Letters of Commendation from several consulting clients praising services
3. Letter from National Association of Registered Dietitians documenting participation in organization
4. Letter of Reference from clinical supervisor

STAR PORTFOLIO CONTENTS 23

COLLEGE MAJOR: **Economics/MBA Finance**
OBJECTIVE: **Financial Management**

■ SKILLS

1. Analyzing financial data (Sample credit reports on individuals/businesses)

2. Managing portfolios (Increased resources by 15% for 3 consecutive years; portfolio performance report)

3. Committee presentations (Programs from presentations)

4. Customer relations (Increased management of funds by $10M: year-end financial report)

■ TRAINING

1. B.A. in Economics/Political Science (Degree)

2. M.B.A./Master's in Business Administration (Degree)

3. Certified Financial Analyst (Association for Financial Analysts)

4. Deming Quality Seminar (Certificate)

■ ACCOMPLISHMENTS

1. Promotion to assistant vice president (Letter from president)

2. Bonuses and vacation trips for performance (Letters)

3. High percentage rate of loan approvals (Statistical report)

4. Increase of $35 million over 3-year period (Report)

■ REFERENCES

1. Letter of Commendation from executive vice president recognizing portfolio growth

2. Letter of Reference from supervisor indicating managerial strengths

3. Letter of Reference from colleague indicating team management approach

4. Letter of Commendation from customer regarding portfolio

STAR PORTFOLIO CONTENTS 24

COLLEGE MAJOR: **Electrical Engineering**
OBJECTIVE: **Quality Engineering/Technical Support**

■ SKILLS

1. Troubleshooting (Description of projects)

2. Research (Analysis, summations, grants written)

3. Team leadership (Agenda/meeting minutes)

4. Training (Syllabus created for course taught as adjunct instructor at local college)

■ TRAINING

1. B.S. in Electrical Engineering (Degree, summa cum laude)

2. Samples (Microsoft Windows 95 Office Suite)

3. Professional Engineer license (License)

4. Professional organization membership letter and list of speakers' topics (Meetings and luncheons attended)

■ ACCOMPLISHMENTS

1. Database and informational forms created

2. Inspection Reports improved product quality following intervention

3. Quality Assurance Reports demonstrating failure rate of less than 0.01% for redesigned product

4. Electrical Engineering National Honor Society (Certificate)

■ REFERENCES

1. Department supervisor (Letter of Reference delineating quality and impact of research conducted)

2. Former department supervisor (Letter of Reference acknowledging training and team building abilities)

3. Department chairperson (E-mail recognizing superior contribution and communication skills)

4. Local chapter president of Engineering Society (Letter of introduction noting organizational leadership)

STAR PORTFOLIO CONTENTS 25

COLLEGE MAJOR: **Electronics**
OBJECTIVE: **Technical Support/Repair**

■ SKILLS

1. Troubleshooting complex electronic circuits (Inventory of repaired circuit boards)
2. Performing accurate calibration procedures
3. Planning and implementing preventive maintenance programs (Schedule of recommended maintenance for problem areas)
4. Installing electronics equipment

■ TRAINING

1. Specialized Electronics Technology with high honors (Diploma)
2. OSHA Health and Safety certification (Certificate)
3. Schematic reading workshop (Certificate)
4. Advanced Computer Repair seminar (Certificate)

ACCOMPLISHMENTS

1. Developed accurate calibration for DM-2 thickness gauge (List of equipment calibrated)
2. Created from conception fully equipped service shop for repair of electronic cash registers (Photographs, layout, and business name application)
3. Instituted preventive maintenance program for service contract customers (Manual)
4. Passed Electronics Technician Associated Training Program (Certificate)
5. Received State Champion Finalist Award (Certificate)

REFERENCES

1. Director of technology (Letter of Reference noting maintenance skills)
2. Satisfied customers (Letters of Commendation regarding diagnostics and repair services)

STAR PORTFOLIO CONTENTS 26

COLLEGE MAJOR: **Elementary Education**
OBJECTIVE: **Elementary Teaching**

■ SKILLS

1. Teaching skills (Evaluations from supervisor, child/parent feedback)
2. Public speaking skills (Evaluations, presentation materials)
3. Interpersonal/relationship skills (Performance evaluations)
4. Administrative skills (Copies of reports, sample records)
5. Community outreach skills (Involvement in church groups, athletic leagues, civic/volunteer work)

■ TRAINING

1. Instructional II Certification (Teaching Certification)
2. Postgraduate courses (Transcripts)
3. Staff development (Ongoing; certificates of attendance/completion)
4. Psychological test administration and evaluation (Record of training hours, evaluation from trainer)

■ ACCOMPLISHMENTS

1. Kappa Delta Pi Education Honor Society (Membership)
2. *Who's Who Among American Colleges & Universities* (Selection)
3. Graduated summa cum laude (Honorary achievement, diploma)
4. Scholarship recipient (Listing of scholarships received)
5. Dean's list (Academic transcripts, news clippings)

■ REFERENCES

1. Letter of Reference from student teacher supervisor (Responsible, creative, good with children)
2. Letter of Reference from director of psychological services (Excellent performance evaluation)
3. Letter of Reference from elementary school principal (Highly competent, effective)
4. Letter of Reference from office administrator (Employer evaluation: highly dependable and efficient)

STAR PORTFOLIO CONTENTS 27

COLLEGE MAJOR: **Engineering**

OBJECTIVE: **Design Engineer**

■ SKILLS

1. Computer Skills (Samples of software)
2. Drawing Skills (Samples of drawing)
3. Detail-oriented (Supervisor evaluation)
4. Creativity (Samples of projects)

■ TRAINING

1. Credits earned toward a B.S. in Engineering (Transcript)
2. Computer courses (List of courses)
3. ROTC (U.S. Navy)

■ ACCOMPLISHMENTS

1. Perfect attendance award (Certificate)
2. Military training (List of completed courses and certificates)
3. Certified lifeguard (Certificate)
4. Emergency Medical Technician (Certificate)
5. Scholarship recipient (Award letter)

■ REFERENCES

1. Letter of Personal Reference from minister
2. Letter of Commendation from superintendent
3. Letter of Reference from former employer
4. Letter of Reference from professor

STAR PORTFOLIO CONTENTS 28

COLLEGE MAJOR: **English**

OBJECTIVE: **District/Regional Sales Manager**

■ SKILLS

1. Marketing (Map of site acquisitions)
2. Training (Trainees' history of advancement)
3. Customer Service (Customer service survey with 70% voluntary response, 93% satisfaction)
4. Management (History of appointments to larger territories and greater responsibilities)

■ TRAINING

1. Sales Enterprises Management Training Program (Certificate)
2. Dale Carnegie Management (Certificate)
3. Dale Carnegie Human Resources (Certificate)
4. Total Quality Management (Letter of Completion)

■ ACCOMPLISHMENTS

1. Press release reporting results of national sales contest
2. Photographs of point of sale displays with sales results
3. Overlay maps of territory reorganization with increased production results
4. Employee retention histories showing retention of 85% of employees for 5+ years
5. Newspaper Photograph (Candidate and local mayor promoting community activity)

■ REFERENCES

1. District Manager (Letter of Reference praising ability to get along with employees and customers)
2. Regional Vice President (Letter of Reference identifying sales, marketing and management accomplishments)
3. Customer (Letter of Commendation requesting more product because of success of promotions)

STAR PORTFOLIO CONTENTS 29

COLLEGE MAJOR: **English Education**

OBJECTIVE: **Teaching/Advising**

■ SKILLS

1. Good communication skills (Examples of papers and presentation materials)
2. Teamwork to cooperate and work well with people (Evaluations)
3. Drama skills (Videotapes of performances)
4. Editing/grammar skills (Copies of edited materials, writing)
5. Writing/reading skills (Performance evaluations, grades)

■ TRAINING

1. B.S. in English Education (Degree)
2. Student teaching (Documentation and performance appraisal by supervisor)
3. Pre-student teaching II (Documentation and performance appraisal by supervisor)
4. Pre-student teaching I (Documentation and performance appraisal by supervisor)

■ ACCOMPLISHMENTS

1. Outstanding English major (Nomination)
2. NCTE Officer (Membership and elections)
3. Peer mentor officer (Membership and election)
4. School Board director (Board minutes)
5. Commendation from fire department

■ REFERENCES

1. Student teacher advisor (Evaluations, letters of recommendation)
2. Pre-student teacher advisor (Evaluations, letters of recommendation)
3. Chief of police (Letter of Personal Recommendation emphasizing character and integrity)

STAR PORTFOLIO CONTENTS 30

COLLEGE MAJOR: **Environmental Science and Management**

OBJECTIVE: **Environmental Science and Safety Manager**

■ SKILLS

1. Scheduling, preparing, and presenting environmental programs
2. Leading hikes and tours of wetland areas
3. Making presentations to high school science classes
4. Operating sonication and gas chromotograph machines
5. Collecting and photographing

■ TRAINING

1. B.S. in Environmental Science (Degree)
2. Department of Environmental Protection Wetlands Course (Certificate)
3. Rural Abandoned Mines Wetlands Reclamation (Seminar program)
4. Bureau of Mines seminar (Certificate)

■ ACCOMPLISHMENTS

1. *Who's Who Among American Students* (Certificate)
2. American Chemical Society (Membership)
3. Dean's list (Certificate)
4. President of Chemical Club (Membership)

■ REFERENCES

1. Letter of Reference (Professor of environmental science, noting breadth of knowledge)
2. Letter of Reference (Professor of hydrogeology, noting field work)
3. Letter of Reference (Supervisor, noting leadership qualities)

STAR PORTFOLIO CONTENTS 31

COLLEGE MAJOR: **Geology**

OBJECTIVE: **Environmental Engineering**

■ SKILLS

1. Computer skills/projects (List of projects designed and computer software developed)

2. Communication skills (List of countries related to extensive worldwide travel for business)

3. Research (Samples of research projects)

4. Instructor (Samples of developed classes and procedural manuals)

5. Supervisor (Responsible for training new employees, department head)

■ TRAINING

1. B.S. in Geology (Degree with honors)

2. B.S. in Environmental Engineering (Degree with highest honors)

3. In-house training (Certificates)

4. Currently enrolled in a master's program (Transcript)

■ ACCOMPLISHMENTS

1. Employee of the Month (Award)

2. Developed procedural manual used by company (Copy of manual)

3. Customer service award (Certificate)

4. Sales award (Certificate)

5. Fluent in four languages (Samples of letters and manuals)

■ REFERENCES

1. Letter of Reference (Emphasizing customer service)

2. Letter of Reference (Enumerating foreign language skills)

3. Letter of Personal Recommendation (Personal reference)

4. Letter of Personal Recommendation (Acknowledging field skills)

STAR PORTFOLIO CONTENTS 32

COLLEGE MAJOR: **History**

OBJECTIVE: **Project/Support Management**

■ SKILLS

1. Operations (Production schedules for 68 employees, samples attached)

2. Purchasing (Procurement flow chart for monthly inventory purchasing and upgrades)

3. Budgeting (Budget with proposed revisions for updating services)

4. Client relations (Survey of client needs and satisfaction)

■ TRAINING

1. B.A. in History with high honors (Degree)

2. Time management seminar (Certificate)

3. Bulk mail regulations seminar (Company Letter of Completion)

4. Business seminars (List and Certificates)

■ ACCOMPLISHMENTS

1. List of procedural modifications proposed/adopted (Presentation materials)

2. Waste hauling invoice/waste recycling receipt (Chart indicating significant savings)

3. Eliminated external labor contracts (Letter of Praise from vice president of human resources)

4. Corporate Rising Star (Award)

5. Article (Company newspaper, regarding successful operation)

■ REFERENCES

1. Letter of Reference (Current colleague describing quality of operations resulting from purchasing and budgeting decisions)

2. Letter of Reference (Former supervisor describing efficiency in managing people and projects)

3. Letter of Reference (Company business manager noting contributions to budget revision and purchasing improvements)

STAR PORTFOLIO CONTENTS 33

COLLEGE MAJOR: **Hotel/Hospitality Management**

OBJECTIVE: **Hotel-Restaurant Manager**

■ SKILLS

1. Computer skills/projects (Samples of software and projects)
2. Food service (List of skills)
3. Communication (Samples of written documents)
4. Supervision (List of entire restaurant staff)

■ TRAINING

1. A.S. in Hotel Management (Degree)
2. Seminars in management (Certificates)
3. Food service courses (Transcript)
4. Credits earned toward a B.S. degree (Transcript)

■ ACCOMPLISHMENTS

1. Employee of the Month (Award)
2. Award for Service (Plaque)
3. Certification in CPR and first aid (Certificate)
4. Graduated with honors (Letter)
5. Promoted from hostess to manager (Letter)

■ REFERENCES

1. Letter of Reference (Highlighting customer service skills)
2. Letter of Commendation (Thank-you letters from satisfied customers)
3. Letter of Reference (Emphasizing professionalism and dedication to get the job done)
4. Letter of Introduction (Referencing value of friends from Hall of Fame professional basketball player)

STAR PORTFOLIO CONTENTS 34

COLLEGE MAJOR: **Housekeeping Supervision Experience**

OBJECTIVE: **Housekeeping Supervision**

■ SKILLS

1. Organization/scheduling (Schedules and changes noted)
2. Supervision (Developed teams and reward systems)
3. Inventory control (Warehouse control sheets and projected savings)
4. Equipment knowledge/maintenance (List of maintenance skills)
5. Evaluations/purchasing (New equipment ordered and cost savings)

■ TRAINING

1. Supervising training series (Certificate)
2. Custodial staffing and standards seminar (Certificate)
3. Management development course (Certificate)

■ ACCOMPLISHMENTS

1. Maintained efficiency following downsizing (Pre-schedule and post-schedule)
2. Saved money through vendor arbitration (Invoices)
3. Employee of the Month (Award)
4. Team award for outstanding service (Team award)

■ REFERENCES

1. Corporate president (Letter of Commendation for contributions to successful stockholders' meetings)
2. Secretary to president (Letter of Commendation noting organizational skills and efficiency)
3. Supervisor (Letter of Reference noting responsibilities and efficiency)
4. Director (Letter of Commendation to supervisor praising skills and efficiency)

STAR PORTFOLIO CONTENTS 35

COLLEGE MAJOR: **Industrial Arts**

OBJECTIVE: **Maintenance Operations Management**

■ SKILLS

1. Supervision (Staff performance evaluations written and given to staff members)
2. Inventory control (Inventory report indicating lower costs, less storage space needed, and fewer job delays)
3. Interviewing and hiring (Employment applications and job descriptions of persons hired)
4. Organization (Sections of procedure manual developed and implemented)

■ TRAINING

1. Industrial Arts course of study (Description)
2. Maintenance management course (Certificate)
3. Customer management course (Certificate)
4. Supervisory management course (Certificate)

■ ACCOMPLISHMENTS

1. Repair requisitions, work orders, inspection reports (Samples)
2. Repair guide table of contents (Reflecting staff performance of repairs previously outsourced)
3. Annual reviews (Demonstrating quality of work and recognizing savings to the company)

■ REFERENCES

1. Director of facilities (Letter of Reference praising quality and quantity of team performance)
2. Company vice president (Letter of Commendation recognizing impact of preventive maintenance measures)
3. Vendor (Letter of Reference commenting on businesslike fashion of conducting business)
4. Subcontractor (Letter of Reference focusing on quality of interaction, cooperation, and analysis)
5. Manager (Letter of Introduction from prominent architect)

STAR PORTFOLIO CONTENTS 36

COLLEGE MAJOR: **Journalism**

OBJECTIVE: **Public Relations for the Arts**

■ SKILLS

1. Art/design (Sample designs, brochures, covers)
2. Public Relations (Sample PSAs and results)
3. Writing (Sample writing and editing of journals)
4. Technical knowledge (List of computer skills and camera and video expertise)
5. Advertising (Sample ads and list of radio/TV spots)

■ TRAINING

1. Graduate studies in journalism (Transcript registration)
2. B.A. in Creative Writing with high honors (Degree)
3. A.S. in Broadcast Journalism with honors (Degree)
4. Certificate in Graphic Arts (Certificate)

■ ACCOMPLISHMENTS

1. Outstanding Award for Writing (2nd place award for journalism)
2. Directed a $350,000 fundraiser for community group (Article and program)
3. Editor of college newspaper (Samples, Outstanding College Newspaper Award)
4. Doubled income for local arts organization (Statistics)
5. *Who's Who Among Students in American Junior Colleges* (Inclusion)

■ REFERENCES

1. Letter of Personal Recommendation from arts council president (Fundraising)
2. Letter of Reference from supervisor (Efficient and organized)
3. Letter of Praise from patrons (Loved your brochures, ads)
4. Letter of Reference from faculty (College editing/writing)

STAR PORTFOLIO CONTENTS 37

COLLEGE MAJOR: **Labor Relations Management**

OBJECTIVE: **Human Resources/Labor Relations Management**

■ SKILLS

1. Independent project management (Safety Manager project)
2. Planning and implementation (Training schedules and syllabi)
3. Mediation (Grievance reports)
4. Technical writing (Job descriptions and policy manual)

■ TRAINING

1. M.A. in Labor Relations (Degree)
2. B.S. in Psychology (Degree)
3. OSHA Requirements in the Workplace (Certificate)
4. Human Resources and the Internet (Certificate)

■ ACCOMPLISHMENTS

1. Professional and human resources certifications (Certificates)
2. Treasurer, Society for Human Resources Management (List of officers)
3. Negotiated contract (Cover and signature pages of the contract)
4. Created three new jobs (Job descriptions)

■ REFERENCES

1. President of company (Letter of Reference alluding to design and implementation skills)
2. Employees (Letter of Commendation thanking for assistance)
3. Academic dean (Letter of Personal Reference emphasizing character)

STAR PORTFOLIO CONTENTS 38

COLLEGE MAJOR: **Legal Secretarial Specialist**

OBJECTIVE: **Legal Secretary/Paralegal**

■ SKILLS

1. Typing (Timed tests measuring speed and accuracy)
2. Speedwriting (90+, cursive sample of speedwriting next to keyboard copies of finished text)
3. Desktop publishing (Samples of fliers, reports, brochures, and invitations)
4. Business Correspondence (Notes/completed correspondence)
5. Supervision (Supervised 5 employees, "Staff of the Month" Award)

■ TRAINING

1. A.S. Degree, Legal Secretarial (Degree with honors)
2. Software applications (List and samples)
3. Paralegal certificate from community college (Certificate)

■ ACCOMPLISHMENTS

1. Phi Theta Kappa (Honorary Society)
2. Cooperative Education Experience (Evaluation from supervisor)
3. Typing (Samples of briefs from co-op at law office)
4. Member of Legal Office Club (Vice president, membership certificate)
5. Fundraising Chairperson (Article in newspaper regarding events, sales, and monies raised)

■ REFERENCES

1. General manager (Letter of Reference)
2. Regional director (Letter of Reference)
3. Faculty in office administration (Letter of Reference, noting skills)
4. Co-op supervisor at law office (Letter of Commendation regarding work habits and attitude)

STAR PORTFOLIO CONTENTS 39

COLLEGE MAJOR: **Management**
OBJECTIVE: **Sales/Customer Service**

■ **SKILLS**

1. Good communication skills (Prepared and wrote training manual, agenda)
2. Know different features of audio components (List of equipment and setup procedures)
3. Marketing/advertising skills (List of PSAs, fliers, and brochures)
4. Mechanical skills (Computer repair certificate)

■ **TRAINING**

1. B.S. in Business (Degree)
2. Two-year certification from technical school (Sales certificate)
3. Two years of experience in business/marketing (Sales certificate)
4. U.S. Army Reserves/communication unit (Army training certificate)

■ **ACCOMPLISHMENTS**

1. Honor student (Dean's list, national dean's list)
2. Class president (Award and letter from college president)
3. Received award during the Gulf War (Medal)
4. Perfect attendance award (Award)
5. Successful activities showing leadership such as blood drive, career programs, and fundraisers (Articles from college and local papers)

■ **REFERENCES**

1. Former employer
2. College professor in business and marketing
3. Military recommendation (Commanding Officer)
4. Community service director (Outstanding volunteer)

STAR PORTFOLIO CONTENTS 40

COLLEGE MAJOR: **Mathematics**
OBJECTIVE: **Service/Operational Projects Management**

■ **SKILLS**

1. Supervision (Minutes of staff meetings and actions taken on staff recommendations)
2. Workflow management (Reorganization report accepted by supervisor to be promoted to top management)
3. Customer service (Telephone responses, ratings presenting overall satisfaction with service provided)
4. Staff development (Staff training histories, including training performance and benefits of training)

■ **TRAINING**

1. B.S. in Mathematics and Statistics (Degree)
2. Supervision workshop sponsored by company (Certificate)
3. Operations management (Certificate from community college)
4. Business communication (Class description and transcript)

■ **ACCOMPLISHMENTS**

1. Service contracts (Awarded over $3 million on contracts; samples and charts attached)
2. Operations redesign proposal (Accepted into operation; design model attached)
3. Board minutes, acceptance of new procedures (Minutes)
4. Attached a profit and loss statement (90%+ new return increase on products)

■ **REFERENCES**

1. Letter of Reference from vice president of operations (Documents sales increase)
2. Letter of Commendation from board president (Increase in sales)
3. Annual Evaluations from supervisor (Supervisory job performance)
4. Letter of Commendation from Business Communications teacher (Outstanding student)

STAR PORTFOLIO CONTENTS 41

COLLEGE MAJOR: **Mechanical Drafting and Design Technology**

OBJECTIVE: **Drafting-Design**

■ SKILLS

1. Creating and scaling computer-assisted designs (Sample)
2. Blueprint interpretation (Blueprints and explanations)
3. Creating models for presentations (Samples listed and photos)
4. Instructing and training (Video of presentation)

■ TRAINING

1. A.S. in Mechanical Drafting and Design Technology (Degree)
2. Computer-aided drafting certification (Certificate)
3. List of engineering and computer courses (Transcript)

■ ACCOMPLISHMENTS

1. Dean's list (Certificate)
2. Recognition of outstanding drawings from faculty (Award)
3. President of Engineering Club (Certificate)
4. Designed and implemented CAD drawings for community housing project (Attached)

■ REFERENCES

1. Instructor, department head (Letter of Reference noting quality of work and strength of character)
2. Supervisor (Letter of Reference noting work ethic and responsibility)
3. Letter from supervisor documenting CAD ability
4. Faculty Letter of Reference (Documenting discipline and enthusiasm)

STAR PORTFOLIO CONTENTS 42

COLLEGE MAJOR: **Mechanical Engineering**

OBJECTIVE: **Mechanical Engineer**

■ SKILLS

1. Developing and implementing design projects (Laboratory notes)
2. Analyzing and introducing solutions (Business proposal)
3. Planning and organizing quality control (Report to department head describing procedures taken to remedy excess waste problems)

■ TRAINING

1. B.S. in Mechanical Engineering (Degree)
2. Major courses taken (Catalog description)
3. Engineering laboratory teaching assistant (Description of duties)

■ ACCOMPLISHMENTS

1. ROTC first place flight ribbon
2. Revised ISO documents (Copies attached)
3. Identified problem and remedy to product content (Report attached)
4. ROTC certificate of commendation

■ REFERENCES

1. Engineering professor (Letter of Reference emphasizing academic excellence and keen analytical ability)
2. Department supervisor (Letter of Reference regarding technical skills)
3. Engineering laboratory director (Letter of Reference denoting precision and attention to detail)

STAR PORTFOLIO CONTENTS 43

COLLEGE MAJOR: **Nursing**

OBJECTIVE: **Nursing**

■ SKILLS

1. People skills (Letters noting personality)
2. Organizational skills (Maintaining patient information and extensive filing)
3. Communication skills (Samples of written articles and letters)
4. Medical terminology/procedures (Samples of test results, list of procedures)

■ TRAINING

1. A.S. in Nursing with highest honors (Degree)
2. B.S. in Business Administration with honors (Degree)
3. M.S. in Nursing (Degree, sample of research)
4. Member of American Nurses Association (Membership certificate)

■ ACCOMPLISHMENTS

1. Registered Nurse (License)
2. Certifications with the Red Cross (Certificates)
3. Volunteer Service Award (Certificate)
4. Dean's list (Certificate)
5. Employee of the Month recognition (Certificate)

■ REFERENCES

1. Letter of Reference (Noting professionalism)
2. Letter of Commendation (Thank-you letters from patients)
3. Letter of Reference (Emphasizing work ethic and knowledge of job performed)
4. Letter of Reference (Highlighting personality and volunteer service)

STAR PORTFOLIO CONTENTS 44

COLLEGE MAJOR: **Occupational Therapy Assistant**

OBJECTIVE: **C.O.T.A.**

■ SKILLS

1. Computer (Used as patient communication device and for photos)
2. Fluent in Spanish (Sample letter written in Spanish to relative in Spain)
3. Splinting skills (List and photographs of splints actually used on patients)
4. Communication, oral and written (Inservice presentations, letters from supervisors and faculty)

■ TRAINING

1. A.S. in Occupational Therapy Assistant (Degree and transcript)
2. CPR Certification (Current certificate)
3. Neurodevelopmental treatment (Training class transcript)
4. Visual perception (Training class transcript)

■ ACCOMPLISHMENTS

1. Certified Occupational Therapy Assistant (A.O.T.C.B. certification)
2. C.O.T.A. Licensure (State of PA license attached)
3. National Dean's list (2 years, 4 letters attached)
4. *Who's Who Among Students in American Junior Colleges* (Certificate attached)

■ REFERENCES

1. O.T.A. work supervisor (Letter of Reference recognizing outstanding work as an O.T. Aide)
2. O.T.A. program faculty (Letter of Reference documenting learning ability)
3. Fieldwork supervisor level I (Letter of Reference documenting skills and teamwork)
4. Fieldwork supervisor level II (Letter of Reference documenting OT skills and teamwork)

STAR PORTFOLIO CONTENTS 45

COLLEGE MAJOR: **Operations Experience**
OBJECTIVE: **Operations/Training Management**

■ SKILLS

1. Marketing (Map of site acquisitions)
2. Training (Trainees' history of advancement)
3. Customer service (Customer service survey with 70% voluntary response, 93% satisfaction)
4. Management (History of appointments to larger territories and greater responsibilities)

■ TRAINING

1. Sales Enterprises Management training program (Certificate)
2. Dale Carnegie Management (Certificate)
3. Dale Carnegie Human Resources (Certificate)
4. Total Quality Management (Letter of Completion)

■ ACCOMPLISHMENTS

1. Press release reporting results of national sales contest
2. Photographs of point of sale displays with sales results
3. Overlay maps of territory reorganization with increased production results
4. Employee retention histories showing retention of 85% of employees for 5+ years
5. Newspaper photograph (Candidate and local mayor promoting community activity)

■ REFERENCES

1. District manager (Letter of Reference praising ability to get along with employees and customers)
2. Regional vice president (Letter of Reference identifying sales, marketing, and management accomplishments)
3. Customer (Letter of Commendation requesting more product because of success of promotions)

STAR PORTFOLIO CONTENTS 46

COLLEGE MAJOR: **Pharmacy**
OBJECTIVE: **Pharmacist**

■ SKILLS

1. Thorough knowledge of drug interactions and side effects (State license, letters of thanks from medical doctors)
2. Research skills (Research publications)
3. Computer skills (Recent course transcript)
4. Supervisory skills (List of five positions supervised)
5. Customer service skills (Increased sales over a 5-year period, annual sales reports)

■ TRAINING

1. B.S. in Pharmacy (Degree)
2. Pharm.D. (Degree)
3. Pharmacy license (License)
4. Pharmacology Seminars & Workshops (Lists and certificates)

■ ACCOMPLISHMENTS

1. Computerized pharmacy department (Sample printouts)
2. Developed pharmacy newsletter to customers (Sample)
3. Journal articles on drug side effects (List of articles)
4. Customer service award (Article in local newspaper)
5. Consultant to pharmaceutical company (Contract)

REFERENCES

1. Letter of Reference from pharmacy faculty member indicating research skills
2. Letter of Reference from medical doctors noting skill in giving advice on medicines
3. Letters of Praise from satisfied customers
4. Letter of Commendation from nursing home supervisor for work with the elderly

STAR PORTFOLIO CONTENTS 47

COLLEGE MAJOR: **Physical Therapist**

OBJECTIVE: **Physical Therapist**

■ SKILLS

1. Assessment of patient medical history/condition (Patient assessments)
2. Development and implementation of treatment plans (Sample treatment plans)
3. Therapeutic exercises/endurance training skills (List of exercises and equipment used)
4. Physical manipulation skills of joints/muscles (Letters from patients)
5. Small business skills (Business plan)

■ TRAINING

1. B.S. in Biology with honors (Degree)
2. M.S. in Physical Therapy (Degree)
3. Licensed Physical Therapist (State license)
4. CPR Certification (Current certificate)

■ ACCOMPLISHMENTS

1. Supervisor of PT staff (Hospital monthly newsletter)
2. Teacher of PT classes at local college (Syllabi of courses, course evaluations)
3. State association vice president (Award)
4. Speaker at national PT association (Programs)
5. Annual evaluation (Copy of evaluations)

■ REFERENCES

1. Letter from state associate for outstanding contribution to Physical Therapy
2. Letter of Commendation from associates regarding physical therapy skills
3. Letter of Reference from director at hospital regarding commitment to service
4. Letter of Reference from dean of allied health regarding supervisor teaching skills

STAR PORTFOLIO CONTENTS 48

COLLEGE MAJOR: **Psychology**

OBJECTIVE: **Chemical Dependency Counselor**

■ SKILLS

1. Counseling/psychotherapy (List of diagnoses, methods, number of clients, and evaluations from supervisor and clients)
2. Supervision (Trained 14 interns: Letters of Appreciation)
3. Assessment (Sample clinical evaluations for three clients)
4. Administration (Attached programs directed for families and seniors)
5. Cross-culture counseling (Peace corps volunteer in Africa for 2 years, certificate and letters)

■ TRAINING

1. M.A. Clinical Psychology (Degree)
2. B.A. Psychology/Philosophy (Degree)
3. National Board of Certified Counselors (Certificate)
4. Drug and alcohol rehab counseling (Certificate)

■ ACCOMPLISHMENTS

1. National Dean's list, Dean's list (Awards)
2. Articles published concerning rehab center (Articles)
3. Programs planned and implemented (Articles, programs, statistics)
4. Association of Black Psychologists (Certificate)
5. Community service leader (Certificate of Outstanding Service from major corporation)

■ REFERENCES

1. Intern supervisor (Letter of Reference from supervisor indicating superior counseling and people skills)
2. Work supervisor (Letter of Reference concerning work)
3. Peace Corps supervisor (Letter of Commendation for outstanding service)
4. Faculty (Letter of Reference in strong support of counselor training and skills)

STAR PORTFOLIO CONTENTS 49

COLLEGE MAJOR: **Psychology**

OBJECTIVE: **Fundraiser**

■ SKILLS

1. Training volunteers (List of non-profit and human service organizations with over 500 volunteers trained to solicit donations)
2. Writing grant proposals (Samples of three award-winning grants)
3. Planning special events (Programs of over 50 events planned and implemented)
4. Organizing direct mail campaigns (Sample letters and computer follow-ups)
5. Management skills (List of 12 major campaigns and contributions)

■ TRAINING

1. B.S. in Psychology with honors (Degree)
2. Certified Fundraising Executive (Credential)
3. Seminar in corporate fundraising (Certificate)
4. Workshop in non-profit fundraising (Program)

■ ACCOMPLISHMENTS

1. Special event for children (Program, funds raised, articles in newspaper)
2. $5 million fundraiser for non-profit organization (Story in local papers)
3. Award for raising major gifts from corporations (Award from university)
4. Developed active Alumni Association (Calendar of events, programs, Letters of Praise)
5. Achievement awards (Awards)

■ REFERENCES

1. Letter of Reference from university president
2. Letter of Reference from non-profit arts and human service organizations
3. Letter of Commendation from corporate sponsor
4. Letter of Appreciation from vice president of children's hospital

STAR PORTFOLIO CONTENTS 50

COLLEGE MAJOR: **Psychology/Education**

OBJECTIVE: **Social Worker**

■ SKILLS

1. Interpersonal/social skills (Supervisor evaluation)
2. Knowledge of psychological theories (Documentation of academic performance, grades, faculty recommendation)
3. Teaching skills (Sample lesson plans, evaluations and class plans, handouts)
4. Speaking/presentation skills (Performance evaluations, satisfaction surveys from audience)
5. Assessment and evaluation skills (Objectives, copies of surveys, research materials and findings)

■ TRAINING

1. B.A. in Psychology/Minor in Education (Degree)
2. Internship at mental health agency (Supervisor evaluation)
3. A.S. in Social Science (Degree)
4. Pre-service training for internship (Certificate of completion; trainer evaluation)

■ ACCOMPLISHMENTS

1. Thesis: "How Alcohol Affects the Brain" (Copy of paper)
2. Brother of the Year, Alpha Chi Rho fraternity, 1994 (Record of service)
3. President of fraternity chapter 1994–1995 (Record of service, accomplishments, duties)
4. Workshop presenter at state conference (Copy of presentation packet)
5. Trainer of new staff at office (Pay raise, supervisor recognition, training materials)

■ REFERENCES

1. Letter of Reference, assistant director of academic advising (Interpersonal skills)
2. Letter of Reference, supervisor from internship (Quality of work, getting along with others)
3. Letter of Reference, psychology professor, university (Good knowledge base, academic performance)
4. Letter of Reference, psychology professor, community college (Personal and academic growth)

STAR PORTFOLIO CONTENTS 51

COLLEGE MAJOR: **Quantitative Business Analysis/MBA**

OBJECTIVE: **Analysis/Financial Management**

■ SKILLS

1. Evaluation (Comparative cost reports prior to and following implementation of new inventory control procedures)
2. Leadership (Description of committee chair activities)
3. Financial management (Monthly statements)
4. Analysis (Merger/acquisition analysis reports)

■ TRAINING

1. MBA, Harvard University (Degree)
2. B.S. in Business (Degree with honors)
3. Sales and marketing strategies (Certificate)
4. Post-graduate computer courses in Word, Peachtree, and Excel (Transcripts)

■ ACCOMPLISHMENTS

1. Newspaper article ($800,000 fundraising project)
2. Spreadsheet (Purchasing/inventory records)
3. National Honor Society in Business Administration (Certificate)
4. Receipt of "Top Gun" Sales Award of the Year (Award)

■ REFERENCES

1. Dean of interfraternity affairs (Letter of Reference emphasizing leadership qualities)
2. Dean of business school (Letter of Reference describing financial analysis/management skills)
3. Sales manager (Letter of Reference recognizing sales and leadership skills)
4. Business manager (Letter of Reference acknowledging assistance in analyzing financial data)

STAR PORTFOLIO CONTENTS 52

COLLEGE MAJOR: **Retail Management**

OBJECTIVE: **Buyer/Retail Merchandising**

■ SKILLS

1. Computers (Database of customers, access)
2. Communications (Monthly reports)
3. Management (Managed office and trained sales staff—Letter of Praise)
4. Languages (Fluent in French and Spanish—Certificate from Spain)
5. Buying (Internship with buyer—Evaluation report)

■ TRAINING

1. A.S. in Retail Management (Degree)
2. B.A. in Business/Accounting (Degree)
3. Fashion Design and Illustrator certificate (Certificate)
4. Certification in Computer Information Systems (Certificate)

■ ACCOMPLISHMENTS

1. Created and directed local talent shows (Programs and advertisements)
2. Sales award for highest annual sales (Award)
3. Dean's list award for high honors (Award)
4. Telemarketing award for 3rd highest monthly sales (Letter)

■ REFERENCES

1. Supervisor of telemarketing (Letter of Reference commending sales ability)
2. Counselor at job center (Letter of Reference regarding work skills)
3. Bank supervisor (Letter of Reference commenting on office and people skills)
4. Retail faculty member (Letter of Reference describing ability to lead and motivate others)
5. Internship supervisor (Letter of Introduction predicting expected future success as a buyer/assistant buyer)

STAR PORTFOLIO CONTENTS 53

COLLEGE MAJOR: **Secondary Education**
OBJECTIVE: **Investigation/Loss Prevention**

■ SKILLS

1. Theft reduction through prevention (Written analysis of fraud detection, including balance sheets and annual reports)
2. Organized security program (Training manual, outline of corporate security program)
3. Administered policies and procedures (Supervision reports of inflation into organized crime operations)
4. Conducted investigations (Annotated list of solved investigations)

■ TRAINING

1. State Police Academy (Graduation certificate)
2. Undergraduate criminal justice courses (Transcript)
3. Criminal investigations seminar (Certificate)
4. Economic crime training (Certificate)

ACCOMPLISHMENTS

1. Solved malt beverage industry case leading to "Born-On Dating" (Newspaper article)
2. Settled largest theft by deception case in commonwealth history (Newspaper article)
3. Received Variety Club law enforcement award (Award)
4. Provided evidence leading to conviction of corrupt judge (Listing of 26-charge indictment)

■ REFERENCES

1. State Policy Commission's Commendation
2. State Attorney General (Letter of Commendation)
3. Victim's relative (Letter of Commendation noting compassion and professionalism)
4. Police captain (Letter of Reference denoting administration and leadership capabilities)

STAR PORTFOLIO CONTENTS 54

COLLEGE MAJOR: **Secretarial Science**
OBJECTIVE: **Office Administrative Support**

■ SKILLS

1. Computers (Programming samples, including database management)
2. Word processing (70+ WPM, straight and statistical test results)
3. Desktop publishing (Posters, fliers, and book, samples)
4. Writing/editing (Copy of monthly newsletter and edited report to executive board)

■ TRAINING

1. Computer training (Certificate)
2. Business Management/Accounting courses (Transcript)
3. A.S. in Secretarial Sciences (Degree)
4. Company training (Certificate from internship)
5. Laboratory Assistant/Instructor (Certificate)

■ ACCOMPLISHMENTS

1. Dean's list/*Who's Who in American Junior Colleges* (Award)
2. Created and edited monthly newsletter for 250-member company (Sample page)
3. National award for newsletter competition (3rd place award)
4. Merit Scholarship recipient (Certificate)

■ REFERENCES

1. Company president (Letter of Reference)
2. Newsletter members (Letter of Praise)
3. Office administrative faculty (Letter of Reference noting skills and ability to learn)
4. Vice president/treasurer (Letter of Reference regarding team and quality management skills)

STAR PORTFOLIO CONTENTS 55

COLLEGE MAJOR: **Speech Pathology**

OBJECTIVE: **Speech Pathologist/Audiologist**

■ **SKILLS**

1. Evaluating patients (Sample evaluation forms)
2. Treating patients (Treatment plans for a variety of clients)
3. Computer skills (Sample computer programs and reports)
4. Treating children (High evaluations for 6 years in children's unit)
5. Treating adults (Recognized by many direct referrals and letters from medical personnel)

■ **TRAINING**

1. M.S. in Speech Language Pathology and Audiology (Degree)
2. B.S. in Biology with high honors (Degree)
3. State licenses (Certification numbers and dual certification)
4. 15 workshops on oral motor skills/aging/etc. (List and Certificates)

■ **ACCOMPLISHMENTS**

1. Article on treatment for children who stutter (Publications)
2. Several clients with traumatic injuries who dramatically improved (Article in newspaper)
3. Invention for detecting early hearing loss (Sample, photos, instructions)
4. Appreciation award from PTO (Award)
5. Patients' letter of thanks (38 letters)

■ **REFERENCES**

1. Letter of Reference from hospital director supporting outstanding service in treating children and adults.
2. Letter of Reference from doctor who made referrals
3. Letter of Commendation from A.S.H.A.
4. Letter of Recommendation from supervisor documenting skills

STAR PORTFOLIO CONTENTS 56

COLLEGE MAJOR: **Teacher Education**

OBJECTIVE: **Teaching**

■ **SKILLS**

1. Clerical skills (Samples of maintained databases and records)
2. People skills (Personal and professional letters noting personality)
3. Computer skills (Samples of brochures, documents, Web pages, and books created)
4. Communication skills (Sample speeches and written letters)
5. Work with children (Letters emphasizing attentiveness)

■ **TRAINING**

1. A.S. in Liberal Arts and Sciences (Degree)
2. Credits earned toward a B.S. in Education (Transcripts)
3. American Red Cross certifications in CPR/Babysitting (Certificates)
4. Training classes for computer applications (Certificates)

■ **ACCOMPLISHMENTS**

1. Perfect attendance (Award)
2. Certified tutor with the Greater Pittsburgh Literacy Council (Certificate)
3. Volunteer honor (Award)
4. Phi Theta Kappa Honorary (Certificate)

■ **REFERENCES**

1. Letter of Reference from vice president of company (Noting dedication and work ethic)
2. Letter of Reference (Highlighting organizational skills)
3. Letter of Reference from day care manager (Emphasizing patience)
4. Letter of Reference from volunteer supervisor (Emphasizing creativity)

STAR PORTFOLIO CONTENTS 57

COLLEGE MAJOR: **Technical Communications**

OBJECTIVE: **Technical Writer**

■ SKILLS

1. Computer skills (Examination score reports)
2. Writing skills (Samples of articles, books, and technical journals)
3. Editorial skills (User document for medical devices)
4. Technical skills (List of technical articles converted into "layman's" English)
5. Scientific skills (Sample manuals and tutorials)

■ TRAINING

1. M.S. in Information Science (Degree)
2. B.S. in Technical Communications (Degree with high honors)
3. A.S. in Computer Science (Degree with high honors)
4. Technical workshops and seminars (List of certificates)

■ ACCOMPLISHMENTS

1. Ultrasound manual (Sample)
2. Adjunct Professor in Technical Writing at local college (Course outline, evaluations)
3. Articles published (List of articles)
4. Company award for outstanding manual conversion to simple terms (Award)
5. Computer tutorial program written for employees (Sample training guide)

■ REFERENCES

1. Letter of Reference from previous supervisor documenting scientific and technical skills
2. Letter of Reference from academic dean documenting teaching skills
3. Letter of Commendation from current supervisor/vice president documenting creativity and writing skills
4. Letter of Commendation from Technical Writers' Guild documenting contributions to the profession

STAR PORTFOLIO CONTENTS 58

COLLEGE MAJOR: **Visual Communications**

OBJECTIVE: **Visual Artist/Designer/Illustrator**

■ SKILLS

1. Quality graphics creation (Samples including layout and design of educational/training multimedia, video games, cover art, and instructional manuals)
2. Imaginative concepts (Descriptions and samples of representative designs, conceptual illustrations)
3. Original art (List of media and samples including traditional and 3-D illustrations and designs)
4. Proficiency in production software (List and samples of operating systems and production software)

■ TRAINING

1. A.S. in Specialized Technology (Degree)
2. Computer animation course (Transcript)
3. Creative writing courses (Transcripts)
4. Advanced photography workshop (Certificate)

■ ACCOMPLISHMENTS

1. CD-ROM graphics samples demonstrating animation and editing tool detective
2. Storyboard animations for proposed children's TV show, HTML coding, Web page
3. 3-D model stills
4. Story writing samples of *Bolz* video game created

■ REFERENCES

1. Graphics supervisor (Letter of Reference outlining skills and projects completed)
2. Colleague (Letter of Introduction describing creativity and ability to channel into practical application)
3. Toy company representative (Letter of Commendation noting creativity and quality of work)
4. Client (Project director, Letter of Reference describing dedication and quality of work)

S.T.A.R. Employment Portfolios: Samples and Documents

The contents of the S.T.A.R. Portfolio support your career objectives. Writing a one-word answer to the question, "What do you do?" produces responses such as accounting, service, management, production, and law. Demonstrating items that "Show what you do or use" produces sample budgets, customer surveys, reports, schedules, and contracts. These items portray typical "skills" representations:

- Examination score report from *Technical Communications—Technical Writer* Portfolio (see Example 5.1).
- Computer Assisted Design from *Mechanical Drafting and Design Technology Drafting/Design* Portfolio (see Example 5.2).
- Annotated list of solved investigations from *Secondary Education—Investigation/Loss Prevention* Portfolio (see Example 5.3).
- Presentation evaluation from *English Education—Teaching/Advising* Portfolio (see Example 5.4).

The *Technical Communications* compiler featured applied and technical knowledge skills. Examination score reports establish his competence to service various computer hardware. He demonstrated his portfolio securing freelance jobs that put him into a position to investigate and negotiate with various companies for full-time employment.

This *Drafting/Design* candidate began post-secondary training while working as a truck driver. Upon completion of his studies, he composed a resume and portfolio in preparation for his job search. He responded primarily to word-of-mouth contacts and called employers who had previously employed graduates of his program. He was invited in for several informal interviews during which he presented his portfolio, including computer-assisted design samples. Two employers told him that he was their first interviewee to present a portfolio of his work. Each offered him a job. He accepted the one with the greater opportunity for advancement.

The *Investigative/Loss Prevention* job seeker had an impressive career record with the state police and as a private detective. Retired from the state police, he wanted to continue to work as an investigator. He networked and discovered that insurance companies were having increasing concerns over fraudulent claims. He discovered an insurance company that was expanding its presence in his community. He responded to an advertisement for an investigator/coordinator, referencing his portfolio in his appli-

Example 5.1

P.C. Service Certification

P.C. Service Certification
Examination Score Report

CANDIDATE: BILL JONES

CANDIDATE ID: 16730019   **DATE: February 2, 1998**

REGISTRATION NUMBER: BILL0004   **SITE NUMBER: PAG**

EXAM: P.C. Service Certification

SERIES: 9019

The report below shows your performance in each section for the Macintosh Service Certification test.

Section Analysis	Number of Questions	Number Correct	Percent Correct
1. Using Service Source	8	6	75%
2. Using Apple Service Guides	6	6	100%
3. Using MacTest Pro	8	8	100%
4. Identifying CRT discharge and adjustment procedures	4	3	75%
5. Macintosh computers: Identifying parts and their functions	8	7	87%
6. Mac OS: Identifying and using features; Identifying and solving specific problems	19	19	100%
7. Troubleshooting: Identifying recommended techniques and solving specific problems	19	19	100%
8. Repair: Following recommended procedures	7	7	100%
9. CRT safety: Identifying hazards and safe/unsafe procedures	2	2	100%

cation. He presented his portfolio during his first interview. The interviewer questioned him extensively about a citation annotated in his portfolio about an insurance fraud investigation. After his second interview, he was offered the position and accepted it.

The *Teaching/Advising* applicant wishing to work with children emphasized her presentational skills. We show here a workshop presentation evaluation example. She wished to relocate to another geographic region, so she e-mailed portfolio outlines along with résumés and cover letters to public and private schools that advertised in professional journals and on the Internet. One hundred contacts led to three trips, four interviews, and one offer, which she accepted and negotiated relocation reimbursement.

Example 5.2

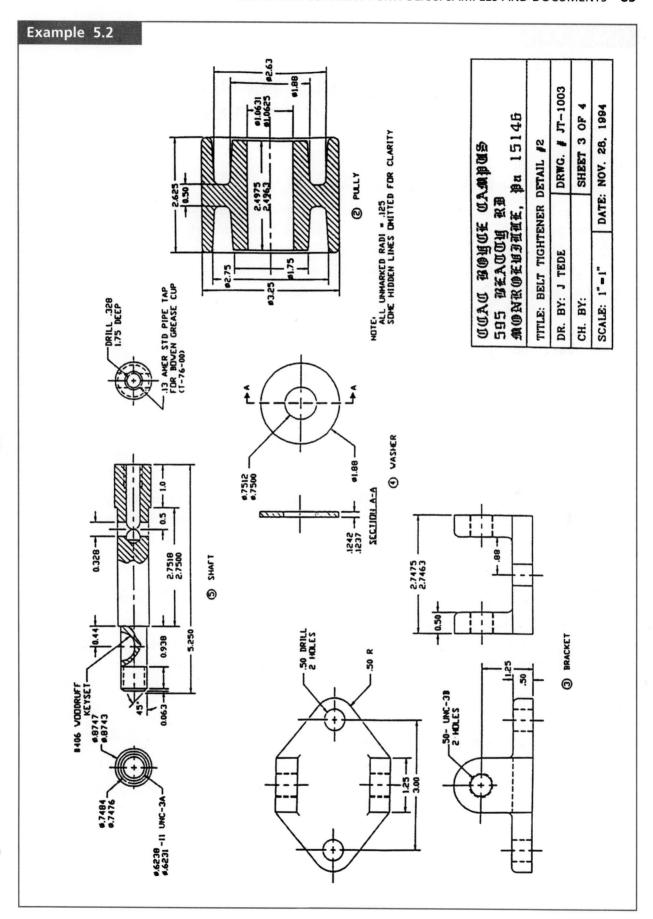

Example 5.3

INVESTIGATION/LOSS PREVENTION
ANNOTATED LIST OF SOLVED INVESTIGATIONS

State Insurance Fraud Investigation, Altoona, PA

The State Insurance regional claims office in Altoona, PA, had been victimized by one of its employees, who had cut fraudulent claim checks to over thirty individuals in several counties. The investigation accomplished with the cooperation of State Insurance audit consultants led to the conviction of 33 individuals and the court-ordered recovery of over $400,000.

Jade County President Judge, Joseph F. Smith prosecution

The investigation led to a Grand Jury indictment against a sitting President Judge, charging him with 76 criminal charges. The ensuing criminal trial lasted over 8 weeks and resulted in the jury returning a guilty verdict.

"Beer Universe" corrupt organization investigation

Selected by the Commissioner of the Pennsylvania State Police to co-direct an 8-man task force. The investigation, which took place in central and western Pennsylvania, eventually led to multiple indictments against four individuals.

Pennsylvania Department of Corrections Ashdon lockdown and investigation

Selected by the Director of the Bureau of Criminal Investigation as part of a task force assembled to interview prison administrators and all of the over 1,000 prison guards at Ashdon Prison in Eastern Pennsylvania. The investigation regarded allegations of corruption.

G & L Specialty Steel Investigation

Investigated a Theft by Deception that took place over a 5-year period. The losses to G & L came to almost $100 million worth of stainless steel products. As part of the disposition in the case, the defendant paid G & L $5.9 million, believed to be the largest restitution ever paid in a criminal matter in Pennsylvania.

Example 5.4

TEACHING CRITICAL READING SKILLS
PRESENTED AT
TRI-STATE READING CONFERENCE
MARCH 25, 1998

	Content	Presentation	Relevance	Overall
Count	29	29	29	29
Stdev +1	10	10	10	10
Avg	9	9	9	9
Stdev –1	8	8	8	8
Max	10	10	10	10
Min	7	5	7	7

TRAINING

The rule of thumb for selecting training representations is "put your best foot forward." If you have strong academic credentials, such as earned advanced degrees, feature them. The *Counseling/Higher Education—Student Services/Administration* portfolio (#20), included, for example:

1. B.A. Degree
2. M.Ed. Degree
3. Ph.D. Degree
4. National Board Certificate (see Example 5.5)

If you're a recent graduate with an initial degree, emphasize academic honors, internships, practicum, and work-study experiences. The *Secretarial Science—Office Administrative Support* portfolio (#54), included, for example:

1. A.S. in Secretarial Sciences
2. scholarship recipient (see Example 5.6)
3. internship
4. laboratory Assistant/Instructor

If you lack formal education, emphasize courses, workshops, seminars, informal education, experience, and on-the-job-training. The *Operations Experience—Operations/Training Management* portfolio (#45), included, for example:

1. Sales Enterprises Management training program (Certificate) (see Example 5.7)
2. Dale Carnegie Management (Certificate)
3. Dale Carnegie Human Resources (Certificate)
4. Total Quality Management (Letter of Completion)

Example 5.5

National Board for Certified Counselors, Inc.

nbcc

Certifies that

Sharon R. Bronstein

has successfully met the professional counseling standards established by the Board and in so doing has earned recognition as a National Certified Counselor (NCC)

NB CC

0279111
Certificate Number

January 29, 1988
Certificate Date

Janine P. Brown
Chairperson

June 30, 2008
Expiration Date

Example 5.6

SCHOLARSHIP AWARD

Presented to

Emma P. Collins

in recognition of exceptional performance and dedicated commitment to the highest standards of excellence in the amount of $2,000.00.

Given By

Merit Scholarship Society

This 3rd Day of *August, 1998*

Heather Rydermann

President

Example 5.7

CERTIFICATION

The National Sales Marketing Association,

in cooperation with

Max Industries, Inc.,

and

American Management Training

Hereby Certify That

Andre B. Zurich, Jr.

has Successfully Completed an Instructional Seminar on Sales Enterprises Management and is Qualified as a

SALES MANAGEMENT SPECIALIST

Kimberlee Cooper
Division Manager

Bill Jones
President

ACCOMPLISHMENTS/AWARDS

Accomplishments either project positive traits such as scholarship, leadership, and courage or reinforce skill competencies. "Honors" accomplishments such as awards, citations, or distinctions are highly desirable. Receipt of a Nobel Prize, Presidential Medal of Honor, or *Time* Person of the Year can go a long way in catching prospective employers' attention. If you have not gained such lofty recognition, more modest forms will do. View examples of "honors" achievements from these portfolios.

1. *Who's Who Among Students in American Junior Colleges* from *Journalism—PR for The Arts* Portfolio (Example 5.8)
2. Dean's List Award for high honors from *Retail Management—Buyer/Retail Merchandising* Portfolio (Example 5.9)
3. Phi Theta Kappa Membership Letter from *Legal Secretarial Specialist—Legal Secretary/Paralegal* Portfolio (Example 5.10)
4. Employee of the Month recognition from *Nursing—Nursing* Portfolio (Example 5.11)

Example 5.8

Who's Who

AMONG STUDENTS IN

American Junior Colleges

This is to certify that

Jennifer Miceki

has been elected to Who's Who Among Students in American Junior Colleges in recognition of outstanding merit and accomplishment as a student at

Community College of Allegheny County

1996–97

H. Freeling Randell

Director

Example 5.9

THE COMMUNITY COLLEGE OF ALLEGHENY COUNTY

presents this

DEAN'S LIST CERTIFICATE

to

Kelly M. McGoug

in recognition of high scholastic achievement at the Community College of Allegheny County during the Fall 1997 Semester.

James C. Smith

James C. Smith, PhD
Vice President of Academic Affairs

Example 5.10

PHI THETA KAPPA

Sigma Omicron Chapter

Dear Honor Student,

It is our pleasure and privilege to inform you that your outstanding academic record makes you eligible for membership in **Phi Theta Kappa,** the International Honor Society of two-year colleges. On behalf of the **Sigma Omicron Chapter** of **Phi Theta Kappa,** chapter advisors Gail Bracken and Linda Neubauer, the officers and members, we extend our congratulations for your academic achievement.

Membership in **Phi Theta Kappa** is a highly coveted honor that will enrich your life while attending the Community College of Allegheny County and will remain with you as you pursue other educational or career goals. We strongly recommend that you take advantage of the opportunity to join this prestigious group of scholars from over 1,100 two-year colleges across the United States, Canada, and abroad. **Phi Theta Kappa** is one of the most respected organizations at the Community College of Allegheny County. Please find enclosed a membership benefit brochure which explains some of the benefits members enjoy.

You are cordially invited to attend an orientation reception in your honor on Friday, February 27, 1998, at 7:00 P.M. in the Student Lounge. If you are unable to attend the reception, an orientation/meeting is scheduled for Sunday, February 22, 1998, at 6:00 P.M. in the Student Lounge. An R.S.V.P. sign-up sheet can be found on the **Phi Theta Kappa** bulletin board located outside of the cafeteria. If you are unable to attend these meetings, please leave a message at the SGA-PTK Office in person or at ext. 1420, and we will contact you. Check out our award-winning chapter Web page at www.acd.CCAC.edu/groups/ptk.

Please plan to attend this reception in order to learn more about this society and what it has to offer you.

Phi Theta Kappa members: You are also receiving a copy of this letter. Please share this information with someone who may be eligible and did not receive a letter.

Sincerely,

Mary Ann Sto

Mary Ann Sto
President, Sigma Omicron Chapter

Enclosure

Dr. Charles Martoni

Dr. Charles Martoni
Dean of Students

CCAC Boyce Campus, 595 Beatty Road, Monroeville, PA 15146

Example 5.11

EMPLOYEE of the MONTH

In appreciation of your fine performance,
we hereby present to

Noreen Faziz

this award recognizing your outstanding productivity
and dedicated service

DUDLEY NURSING HOME

Thomas P. Dudley

President

The ___3rd___ Day of ___March 1997___

Accomplishments are also represented in the form of trade or professional licenses, recognition by employer, industry, or community; work samples, publications, evaluations; and other imaginative entries. View examples of "traditional" achievements from these portfolios.

5. Promotion to Assistant Vice President from *Economics/MBA/Finance—Financial Management* Portfolio (Example 5.12)
6. Golf Events and Dates from *Accounting—Golf Club Manager* Portfolio (Example 5.13)
7. State Champion Finalist Award from *Electronics—Technical Support/Repair* Portfolio (Example 5.14)
8. Schedule C of IRS 1040 from *Business Administration—Production Planning/ Supervision* Portfolio (Example 5.15)

Example 5.12

First Financial Bank 15 Piper Street, Grand Island, Nebraska 68504

May 2, 1998

43 Woodlane Road
Lincoln, NE 68503

Dear John Tack:

Your promotion to Assistant Vice President is effective as of July 1, 1998. Your initiative, staff development, and attention to detail have been noted by your supervisor, who recommended you for promotion. We are pleased to have you on the management team.

Sincerely yours,

Andrew P. Jacko

Andrew P. Jacko, President
First Financial Bank

Example 5.13

Women's Golf Association
EVENTS AND DATES

Date/Day	Event
April 3, Thurs.	Opening Breakfast - 8:45 a.m.
April 10, Thurs.	Event Day
April 17, Thurs.	Ace Day
May 15, Thurs.	Ace Day
May 22, Thurs.	Florida Scrambles
May 25, Sun.	Memorial Day Mixed Event, 1:30 p.m. Shotgun
May 29, Thurs.	Massey Day
June 5, Thurs.	Spring Invitation - 8:30 a.m. Shotgun
June 6, Fri.	Interclub (at St. Clair)
June 2, Thurs.	Flag Day
June 17, Tues.	Trotter Cup
June 19, Thurs.	Trotter Cup
June 22, Sun.	Mixed Event - 1:30 p.m. Shotgun
June 26, Thurs.	Member - Member, 8:00 a.m. Shotgun
July 3, Thurs.	Red, White & Blue Tournament
July 6, Sun.	Independence Day Mixed Event - 1:30 p.m. Shotgun
July 10, Thurs.	Seniors' Tournament
July 11, Fri.	Interclub (at Chartiers)
July 17, Thurs.	Queen Bee - Ace Day
July 24, Thurs.	Queen Bee
July 29, Tues.	Queen Bee - Rain Day
Aug. 1, Fri.	Interclub (at South Hills)
Aug. 2, Sat.	Mixed Invitation - 1:30 p.m. Shotgun
Aug. 7, Thurs.	Club Championship First Round
Aug. 8, Fri.	Club Championship Second Round
Aug. 14, Thurs.	Club Championship Third Round
Aug. 28, Thurs.	Fall Invitation - 8:30 a.m. Shotgun
Aug. 31, Sun.	Labor Day Mixed Event - 1:30 p.m. Shotgun
Sept. 4, Thurs.	Mulligan Day
Sept. 11, Thurs.	Derby Day - 8:00 a.m. Shotgun
Sept. 14, Sun.	Mixed Championship - 1:30 p.m. Shotgun
Sept. 18, Thurs.	Three Queens and a King - 8:00 a.m. Shotgun Ace Day
Sept. 25, Thurs.	Ace Tournament - Final Day of Competition
Oct. 2, Thurs.	Closing Event and Brunch

Example 5.14

PENNSYLVANIA ATHLETIC ASSOCIATION

ATHLETIC AWARD

STATE CHAMPIONSHIP FINALIST

Bill Jones

of

PA Community College

competed in the Pennsylvania State Collegiate Championship in the sport of Tennis

for the year 1999

Don Johnsen
Commissioner

Peter Samuel
President–WPCC

Billy Jean Queen
President–EPCC

Example 5.15

SCHEDULE C **(Form 1040)** Department of the Treasury Internal Revenue Service (99)	**Profit or Loss From Business** (Sole Proprietorship) ▶Partnerships, joint ventures, etc., must file Form 1065. ▶Attach to Form 1040 or Form 1041. ▶See Instructions for Schedule C (Form 1040).	OMB No. 1545-0074 **1997** Attachment Sequence No. **09**

Name of proprietor **John Bond**   Social security number (SSN) **111 - 22 - 3333**

A   Principal business or profession, including product or service (see page C-1)   **Package Delivery**   B Enter principal business code (see page C-6) ▶

C   Business name. If no separate business name, leave blank.   D Employer ID number (EIN), if any

E   Business address (including suite or room no.) ▶

City, town or post office, state, and ZIP code

F   Accounting method: (1) ☒ Cash   (2) ☐ Accrual   (3) ☐ Other (specify) ▶

G   Did you "materially participate" in the operation of this business during 1997? If "No," see page C-2 for limit on losses . . . . ☒ Yes ☐ No

H   If you started or acquired this business during 1997, check here . . . . ▶ ☐

Part I   Income

1	Gross receipts or sales. Caution: *If this income was reported to you on Form W-2 and the "Statutory employee" box on that form was checked, see page C-2 and check here* . . . . ▶ ☐	1	195,720
2	Returns and allowances	2	4,210
3	Subtract line 2 from line 1	3	191,510
4	Cost of goods sold (from line 42 on page 2)	4	
5	Gross profit. Subtract line 4 from line 3	5	191,510
6	Other income, including Federal and state gasoline or fuel tax credit or refund (see page C-2)	6	
7	Gross income. Add lines 5 and 6 . . . . ▶	7	191,510

Part II   Expenses. Enter expenses for business use of your home only on line 30.

8	Advertising	8	10,200	19	Pension and profit-sharing plans	19	
9	Bad debts from sales or services (see page C-3)	9		20	Rent or lease (see page C-4):		
10	Car and truck expenses (see page C-3)	10		a	Vehicles, machinery, and equipment	20a	
11	Commissions and fees	11		b	Other business property	20b	
12	Depletion	12		21	Repairs and maintenance	21	
13	Depreciation and section 179 expense deduction (not included in Part III) (see page C-3)	13	8,025	22	Supplies (not included in Part III)	22	6,821
14	Employee benefit programs (other than on line 19)	14		23	Taxes and licenses	23	
15	Insurance (other than health) . . .	15	762	24	Travel, meals, and entertainment:		
16	Interest:			a	Travel	24a	
a	Mortgage (paid to banks, etc.) . . .	16a		b	Meals and entertainment		
b	Other	16b		c	Enter 50% of line 24b subject to limitations (see page C-4) .		
17	Legal and professional services	17		d	Subtract line 24c from line 24b	24d	
				25	Utilities	25	
				26	Wages (less employment credits)	26	78,272
18	Office expense	18	18,558	27	Other expenses (from line 48 on page 2)	27	5,282
28	**Total expenses** before expenses for business use of home. Add lines 8 through 27 in columns . . . . ▶					28	127,920
29	Tentative profit (loss). Subtract line 28 from line 7					29	63,590
30	Expenses for business use of your home. Attach Form 8829					30	
31	**Net profit or (loss).** Subtract line 30 from line 29. ● If a profit, enter on Form 1040, line 12, and ALSO on Schedule SE, line 2 (statutory employees, see page C-5). Estates and trusts, enter on Form 1041, line 3. ● If a loss, you MUST go on to line 32.					31	77,650
32	If you have a loss, check the box that describes your investment in this activity (see page C-5). ● If you checked 32a, enter the loss on Form 1040, line 12, and ALSO on Schedule SE, line 2 (statutory employees, see page C-5). Estates and trusts, enter on Form 1041, line 3. ● If you checked 32b, you MUST attach Form 6198.					32a ☐ 32b ☐	All investment is at risk. Some investment is not at risk.

For Paperwork Reduction Act Notice, see Form 1040 instructions.   Schedule C (Form 1040) 1997

JSA
7X0110 2.000

REFERENCES

References are usually expressed in letters. The most common of these is a Letter of Reference that describes your skills and accomplishments. In order to secure letters referencing your skills and accomplishments, you must enumerate these skills and accomplishments and request that the writer address them.

The best Letter of Reference is one drafted by a person in a position of authority who writes well, knows you and your work, thinks highly of you, and expresses that high regard, making positive reference to your priority skills and accomplishments. See the example from the *Mechanical Drafting and Design Technology—Drafting/Design* Portfolio (Example 5.16).

The second best Letter of Reference is one that you have composed and that is signed by a person in a position of authority who knows you and your work, thinks highly of you, and confirms your expressions of high positive regard, referencing your priority skills and accomplishments. See the example from the *Labor Relations—Human Resources/Labor Relations Management* Portfolio (Example 5.17).

Letters of Commendation may be unsolicited, such as in the *Housekeeping Supervision Experience—Housekeeping Supervision* Portfolio, a spontaneous note of appreciation from the company president for a job well done. (see Example 5.18). In the *English—District/Regional Sales Manager* Portfolio, the applicant requested a letter to support her candidacy for advancement (see Example 5.19).

Letters of Introduction should originate from a noted personage or a person in a position of prominence. In the *Hotel Hospitality Management—Hotel/Restaurant Manager* Portfolio, the compiler includes a Letter of Introduction from a Hall of Fame professional basketball player whom he befriended as a fan. The letter speaks to their friendship and the noted player's perception that the most significant reward for playing in the NBA was the opportunity to form such relationships.

The originator of the *Maintenance Operations Management* Portfolio included in his materials a letter from the manager of a prominent architect introducing him to the president of a resort and national builder's supply company (see Example 5.20).

A Letter of Personal Recommendation speaks to an individual's character, conduct, and/or competence in non–work-related performance. See the example from the *English Education—Teaching/Advising* Portfolio (Example 5.21).

Example 5.16

Community College
of Allegheny County

BOYCE CAMPUS
595 Beatty Road
Monroeville, PA 15146-1395
1 (724) 371-8651

www.ccac.edu   September 5, 1999

To Whom it May Concern:

I have known Mr. John L. Hill, social security number 000-123-456, for about four years. In this period of time, I have seen many outstanding and excellent qualities in Mr. Hill, both as a student and an individual.

As a student, Mr. Hill is always cooperative, enthusiastic, and a hard worker. His analytical skills (within the constraints of our technology program) are at the point at which he can perform and solve a wide variety of engineering technology problems. He is the most well disciplined and hard-working student I have had the pleasure of teaching during my tenure as an instructor.

As a person, Mr. Hill has the type of personality and enthusiasm that both employers and fellow employees appreciate. He gets along well with everyone. I feel that he has excellent potential leadership qualities since he has often volunteered quickly when several extra projects and activities have been required. I give him my highest recommendation.

Sincerely,

Joseph M. Smith

Joseph M. Smith, P.E., PLS
Professor of Engineering
Chairman, Engineering Department

Example 5.17

TAC, INC.

April 6, 1998

To Whom it May Concern:

James Judd served as Human Resources Administrator with Triangle Answering Service, Inc., for a period of eighteen months. Mr. Judd began his service in this exempt-level position on January 22, 1996, and terminated on July 21, 1997.

During his tenure, Mr. Judd designed and implemented every facet of our human resources function. His activities included, but were not limited to, the following: created job descriptions; developed a policy manual; designed training, employee orientation, and employee relations programs; and ensured legal compliance where applicable.

Mr. Judd interacted productively with all members of the company. He demonstrated creativity, dependability, and organizational competence. He also demonstrated a keen ability to analyze the specific needs of this company, and provided the necessary guidance in his area of professional expertise. He excels at oral and written presentations and has effectively applied these skills to promote the interests of this organization.

Sincerely,

Eve Spadoni

Eve Spadoni
President, TAC, Inc.

788 Chestnut Avenue, Altoona, PA 16601 814/941-0000

Example 5.18

Gulf Oil Corporation

May 14, 1998

Mr. William P. Brown
1839 Frick Building
Pittsburgh, PA 15222

Dear William:

The 1998 Annual Shareholders' meeting is now over and, according to the comments from a number of shareholders and directors, it was a success. I want to extend my sincere appreciation for your participation and help in making it the success it was.

Sincerely yours,

Robert T. Jones

Robert T. Jones
Chairman of the Board
RTJ/pcc

Robert T. Jones Chairman of the Board   *Investment Building, Pittsburgh, PA 15230*

Example 5.19

4/25/97

To: Caroline Jackson

Cc: Terry Witt   Dominic Carter   Francis Catsen
    Robert Smith   Joseph Bayer   Mary Griff

Fr: Jane Wilks
Re: Your Accomplishments

Of all the marketing managers, you have had the most challenging list to market this year. You have successfully turned around Stoner despite the late instock and the lack of momentum in the fall. At 24,000 copies closed to date, we are sure to hit 50,000 copies. Nobody would have predicted that at the National Sales Meeting.

In data processing, you have worked closely with Gary and the field marketers to demystify the discipline and build confidence in the books. You have been able to mobilize both the field marketers and the managers to make DP a conference call priority.

You have shown tremendous leadership with Griffin to Michele, Whitney and Joyce. When Roland called this morning, he said that your enthusiasm and willingness to help the reps in his region was just what they needed to turn things around. Roland doesn't hand out compliments lightly.

You've also worked very closely with your co-workers to make things happen in all your other areas of responsibility—tax, finance, Excel.

Above all else, you have put your heart and soul into these evening conference calls. You have had more conference calls scheduled than anybody else and you have been indefatigable in your encouragement and coaching of reps. Your attitude, coupled with your determinism and knowledge of what needs to be done, makes things happen. What you've accomplished in this year—and the situations that you have successfully turned around—will enable you to mount any other challenge in the years to come. We're proud of you.

Example 5.20

GGA
ARCHITECTS, INC.
Architects/Planners/Designers

Five Gateway Center
Pittsburgh, PA 15222
412/391-0000

Maggie Jill Smith
Seven Woodland Resort
Rt. 208
P.O. Box 6
Village of Farmington, PA 15438

September 20, 1999

Dear Maggie:

I write with the hope that you will find the enclosed resume of Mr. Bill Jones of some interest to you and to Jim as well.

As you will discover from reading his resume, Bill hails from New England, where he made his career first as a tradesman and then up through the ranks to facilities management positions, with special emphasis on quality control and project scheduling.

Bill now resides in Sewickley and is seeking a position where his skills and experience can be challenged and put to good use.

Bill is a very personable and competent man, and I encourage you and Jim to make his acquaintance as he is especially skilled and interested in the kind of "high design" and complexity of detail that you enjoy.

I am sure that after having met Bill, you will consider him to be a strong candidate for any maintenance operations position that you have a need to fill.

I know how busy and hectic your schedule is and how difficult it can be at times to set a meeting time. Therefore, I have left that job to Bill himself. I have taken the liberty of giving your phone number to Bill so he can contact you in the near future. Please allow him to introduce himself; it will be of benefit to all.

As always,

James T. Kirk

James T. Kirk, AIA

Encl.

Example 5.21

DEPARTMENT OF POLICE

BOROUGH OF GLASSPORT

Glassport, Pennsylvania 15045

Edward Dice	PHONE (412) 555-3921	Patrick Smith
CHIEF OF POLICE		LIEUTENANT—JUVENILE OFFICER

April 24, 1999

To Whom it May Concern:

It is my pleasure to recommend to you Keith Saire. I have known Keith and his family for many years as lifelong residents of Glassport. My every contact with him has shown a man of strong character and deep personal integrity.

Keith has demonstrated his interest in the community and caring for others through many years of service with the borough's fire and ambulance department. Now his leadership qualities are evident in his elected position as School Board Director.

For these reasons I heartily recommend Keith Saire for any situation requiring honesty, energy, persistence, and commitment.

Sincerely,

Edward Dice

Edward Dice
Chief of Police
Borough of Glassport

THE COMPLETE PORTFOLIO

The following pages display representative samples of the *Visual Communications—Visual Artist/Designer/Illustrator* Portfolio. This graphic artist's skills center on his creation of diversified commercial-quality products. In his portfolio, he demonstrates his proficiency with production software through an impressive list of software he has used and representative samples of products created with different software (Example 5.22).

His education consists of an entry-level degree with extensive informal on-the-job training and self-instruction. His formal education, represented by his degree, is applicable to his objective (Example 5.23).

His presentation of original 3-D model stills illustrates creativity, advanced design accomplishments, and a variety of commercial applications, including animated video cartoons, comic strip/book characters, and toys (Examples 5.24a, b, and c).

His letter of commendation from a toy company representative reinforces his claims of creation of commercial-quality graphic merchandise (Example 5.25).

His future plans include placing his entire portfolio onto a CD-ROM and a Web site on the Internet.

Example 5.22

ARTIST/DESIGNER/ILLUSTRATOR PORTFOLIO

Computer/Software Skills

OPERATING SYSTEMS: Macintosh System 8, DOS, Windows 97, Amiga Workbench 3.0

SOFTWARE PROFICIENCY

GRAPHIC SOFTWARE	DESKTOP PUBLISHING	ANIMATION
Photoshop	PageMaker	Animation Stand
Illustrator	Word 97	Animator Pro
FreeHand	QuarkXPress	GIF Builder
Painter		
Image Ready		

VIDEO & SOUND EDITING	3-D SOFTWARE	AUTHORING
Premiere	RAY Dream Studio	Director
Sound Edit	Infini-D	HTML
	Extreme 3-D	Powerpoint
	Dimensions	
	Poser	

Example 5.23

THE ART INSTITUTE OF PENNSYLVANIAN

John Mirenzi

has satisfied the requirements for this Associate in Specialized Technology Degree in the course of

Visual Communications

In representing the Faculty and Officers of The Art Institute, we have directed that our corporate seal be hereunto affixed.

Awarded at Pittsburgh, Pennsylvania

June 14, 1998

Saundra Vandyke
President

John Llinde
Director of Education

William J. McAulty
Academic Department Director

Example 5.24a

Example 5.24b

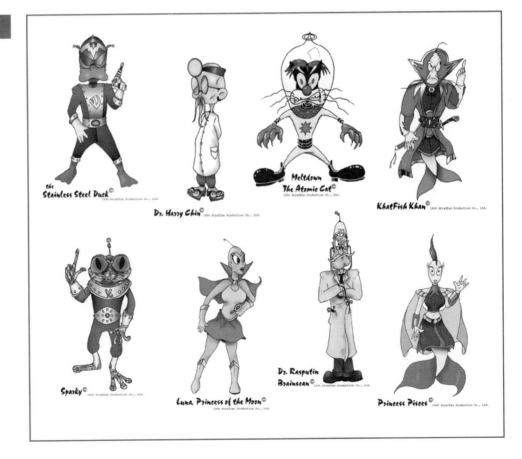

Example 5.24c

Example 5.24c

Continued.

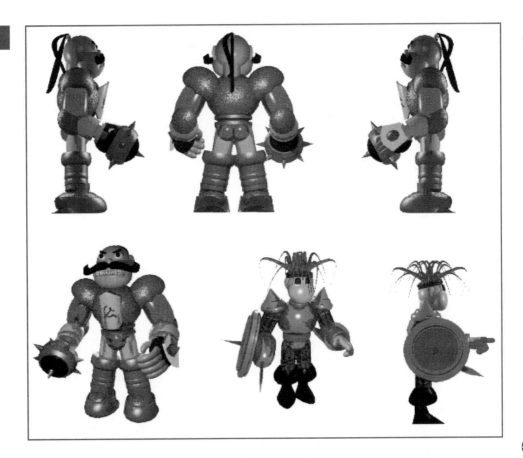

From the CD-ROM "Next Step: Mars?" © IVI Publishing and QED Communications

Example 5.25

H.O.T. Toy Company

123 Fast Lane
Hollywood, CA 90212

April 17, 1999

Mr. John Mirenzi
4587 Pennway Avenue
Apartment 5F
Erie, PA 15066

Dear Mr. Mirenzi:

I have received and reviewed the sketches, interfaces and 3-D models for your proposed CD-ROM video game with the working title of *Stainless Steel Duck*. You have a potentially viable commercial project.

I would be interested in reviewing the completed prototype video game once you have created it.

We are, however, interested in taking on projects to reach a broader market. Thus we seek ideas and licensing rights for production/distribution of toys and other merchandising as well as television and movie productions.

Please keep in touch with me on the developments of this project.

Best wishes,

James Richter

James Richter
Product Development Manager

Three S.T.A.R. Portfolios

6

Three actual S.T.A.R. Employment Portfolios are presented in this chapter with particular uses for marketing each person's needs to employers. The three S.T.A.R. Portfolios are each custom designed for a particular application, as follows.

THREE S.T.A.R. PORTFOLIOS

1. To compete with those people who have in-depth experience in their field (Portfolio One: Donna's)
2. To focus on specialized skills such as management (Portfolio Two: Frank's)
3. To introduce a person's background, competencies, and awards to particular employers (Portfolio Three: Keith's)

HOSPITALITY MANAGEMENT: PORTFOLIO ONE

Donna was a nontraditional student who wanted to change careers due to circumstances in her own life. She needed more money, and she had a desire to work in a creative field as a supervisor or program director. Since Donna's S.T.A.R. Portfolio was completed before she graduated, her actual degree with highest honors, her Outstanding Student of the Year Award, her Outstanding Student of the Year in Hospitality Management Award, and the graduation program listing her as one of the graduation speakers all need to be added to her portfolio. It is evident that her portfolio, even in the short span of one month before graduation, has further developed and expanded. These new materials and documents can easily be added to one of the four sections: Skills, Training, Accomplishments, and References.

Donna will be using her portfolio on her interview to showcase her talents, capabilities, energy, and the quality of her work. By documenting many of her skills and accomplishments, she details the thoroughness of her work, including leadership in school activities. During and after the job interview, the employer will in all probability be searching for ways to hire Donna if a job is available. Even if the employer has no current positions available, he or she will, with Donna's encouragement, be happy to recommend Donna to another company that might need a person with Donna's background. Donna's portfolio begins on page 115.

GOLF MANAGEMENT: PORTFOLIO TWO

The second portfolio is Frank's, a golf professional who is looking for a position as head golf pro at a prestigious country club. Frank has customized his S.T.A.R. Portfolio to center on his golf management skills, assuming correctly that highlighting his training and awards on his résumé will be sufficient. Frank had spiral-bound copies of his portfolio printed for each of the committee members who would be interviewing him for a new position. The portfolio includes a copy of his résumé and a detailed description of three professional areas, including: 1. Managing the Golf Shop, 2. Teaching Golf Lessons and Clinics, and 3. Coordinating Special Events and Tournaments. The S.T.A.R. Portfolio makes an excellent first impression on the committee members. It is a prepared summary that Frank can refer to during the interview, and it presents a neatly formatted package that the committee members can take with them to review on a later occasion. Review Frank's portfolio, which begins on page 164.

HISTORICAL RESTORATION: PORTFOLIO THREE

The third portfolio is Keith's, who has taken up residence in historic Ligonier, a small town outside of Pittsburgh. He had worked in historic preservation and renovation in England. Being new to Pittsburgh and the tri-state area, Keith needed an employment portfolio to showcase his talents. His S.T.A.R. Portfolio first of all described his accomplishments and awards to market himself for job interviews, and presented his background and knowledge of historic preservation and renovation at the actual interview, formal or otherwise. Keith either mailed out his portfolio or visited with professionals and organizations in his field, leaving a copy of his portfolio with them. This specialized edition of Keith's S.T.A.R. Portfolio, which includes detailed photographs and drawings of his projects at various stages of restoration from beginning to completion as well as letters of reference from notable persons and dignitaries, presents an extremely favorable impression at the interview of competence, quality, and artistic design based upon extensive research and knowledge. Keith's portfolio begins on page 185.

Now review the three S.T.A.R. Portfolios. For purposes of space and consistency, we've reformatted examples to follow the layout and design of this text. For purposes of ease of identification, we've used labels for each piece. Your own portfolio should be designed to work with your examples. Labels may or may not be necessary depending upon the nature of the material.

PORTFOLIO ONE

PORTFOLIO PRESENTATION OF DONNA CIPRIANI

This portfolio is the work of Donna Cipriani. Please do not copy without permission. Some exhibits, work samples, and/or service samples are the property of the organization whose name appears on the document. Each has granted permission for this product to be used as a demonstration of my work.

S.T.A.R. PORTFOLIO CONTENTS FOR DONNA CIPRIANI

WORK PHILOSOPHY AND CAREER GOALS

RESUME

SKILLS

- Event Analysis. Theme: "Southwestern Lunch"
- Recruitment Posters
- Works in Progress

TRAINING

- Academic Transcripts
- Courses

AWARDS AND ACCOMPLISHMENTS

- All-Pennsylvania Academic Team
- Dean's List
- All-USA Academic Team
- Phi Theta Kappa
- *Who's Who Among Students in American Junior Colleges*
- All-American Scholar
- Word FM 101.5 in Pittsburgh

LETTERS OF RECOMMENDATION

- Dean of Students
- Program Director, Faculty
- Director of Nursing
- Director of Public Relations
- Program Education Director
- Registered Nurse

WORK PHILOSOPHY AND CAREER GOALS

My parents instilled in me an old-fashioned work ethic. I believe any job should be done to the best of your ability and should be done right the first time. I have attempted to continue this work ethic in any job I have held. I feel that to do a good job, you must take pride in the work that you perform. No matter what the job, you need to learn all the necessary skills to perform it. I know that any job I obtain in the hospitality industry will require knowledge, skill, and leadership qualities. School has given me a good foundation, but real-world work experience will build on that foundation and help me become a true contributor to the organization with which I work.

After graduation, I will seek a position working as a meeting specialist or as a convention coordinator. These positions will allow me to gain experience in various aspects of the hotel/convention area of the hospitality industry. My goals for the future are to obtain my four year degree and eventually to obtain a top management position with a large chain or convention facility.

Donna Marie Cipriani
804 Paulson Drive
Pittsburgh, PA 15235
(724) 555-6999

OBJECTIVE: To obtain a position as a Meeting Specialist or Even Coordinator.

SUMMARY OF QUALIFICATIONS:
- Enthusiastic and energetic.
- Well organized and detail-oriented.
- Strategic planner.
- Self-motivated.
- Independent decision maker.

EDUCATION:
- A.S. Degree in Hotel–Motel Management (May 1998)
- Certificate in Food Service Management (May 1998), Community College of Allegheny County, Boyce Campus, Monroeville, PA
- 3.96 Q.P.A., Dean's list, Phi Theta Kappa member
- Commencement speaker for graduating class of 1998, representing Boyce Campus of the Community College of Allegheny County.

WORK EXPERIENCE:

Assistant Manager and Desk Clerk (1997–1998)
Blue Spruce Motel and Restaurant, Route 22, Murrysville, PA
- Reservations.
- Daily auditing procedures of guest accounts.
- Cooking for snack bar.
- Managing and scheduling 10 employees in the pool snack bar.
- Ordering and receiving supplies.
- Closing procedures for cash registers.

Food Lab Assistant and Student Ambassador of Recruitment (1996–Present)
Community College of Allegheny County, Boyce Campus, Monroeville, PA
- Assisted in the development of a database for student recruitment.
- Created monthly information bulletin boards, free recipe sheets, and ads for closed-circuit television at Boyce Campus.
- Maintained Food Service Lab.
- Assisted in planning, catering, and coordinating events at Boyce Campus.
- Tutored students in Hospitality Department courses.
- Participated in recruitment activities for Community College of Allegheny College, Boyce Campus, for the Hospitality Department.

(continued)

RESUME   Continued.

Nursing Assistant (1976–1995)
McKeesport Hospital, McKeesport, PA

Receptionist and Billing Clerk (1975–1976)
Dr. Alex Hilton, White Oak, PA

Department Manager and Floor Supervisor (1973–1975)
W.T. Grant Co., Duquesne, PA

ACTIVITIES AND MEMBERSHIPS:

Phi Theta Kappa International Honor Society, American Legion Ladies Auxiliary
Culinary Activities:

> Valentine's Day Dinner (48 people), Allied Health Luncheon (25 people) and the Ribbon Cutting Luncheon (300 people), Continental Breakfast Meeting (25 people), Christmas Concert (300 people per night), and Day Care Center Luncheon (30 people).

COMMUNITY AND PUBLIC SERVICE:

- Coordinated, scheduled students, and recruited for Community College of Allegheny County at Great Cake Auction for the Make-A-Wish Foundation on February 27–28, 1998.
- Co-chairperson for Adopt-a-Family Committee and Angel Tree Committee, Phi Theta Kappa service projects for the academic year 1997–1998.
- Cooking and serving at American Legion Ladies' Auxiliary pancake breakfast on April 20, 1997.
- Cooking and serving at the Optimists' Club spaghetti dinner in May 1997.
- Cooking and serving at Port Vue Boro's Fun to Be a Kid Day pancake breakfast on October 19, 1997.
- Creating and editing a cookbook for lower income families who receive food items from the local food bank and area churches.
- Contacting and developing a database of restaurants and suppliers in Allegheny County for the National Restaurant Association, Western Pennsylvania Chapter.

AWARDS AND RECOGNITIONS:

- Dean's list, academic years 1996–1997, 1997–1998.
- Nominated for All-U.S.A. Community & Junior College Academic Team, academic year 1997–1998.
- All-State Pennsylvania Community & Junior College Academic Team, academic year 1997–1998.
- Included in *Who's Who Among Students in American Junior Colleges,* academic year 1997–1998.
- USAA All-American Scholar Collegiate Award.
- Hall of Honor Distinguished Chapter Member for Phi Theta Kappa, academic year 1997–1998.
- Outstanding Female Student, academic year 1997–1998.

References available upon request.

SKILL AND WORK SAMPLES

EVENT ANALYSIS

THEME: "SOUTHWESTERN LUNCH"

TABLE OF CONTENTS

1. Event menu
2. Food cost analysis
3. Laboratory analysis
4. Market purchase form
5. Recipes and cost
6. Production charts
7. Tabletop design
8. Room configuration
9. Inventory list
10. Event specifications

EVENT MENU

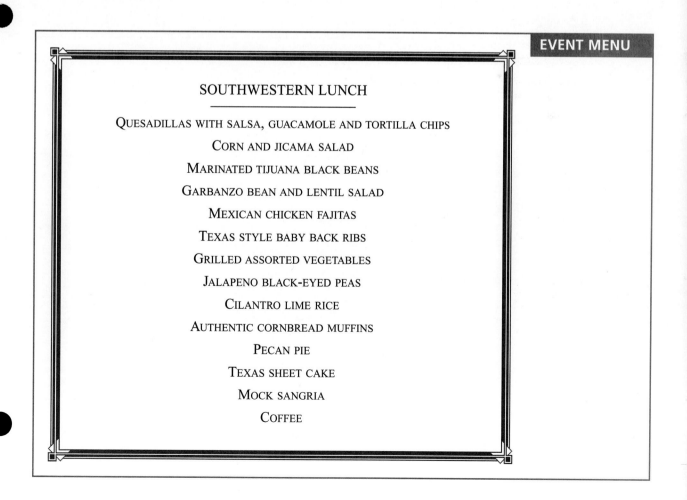

SOUTHWESTERN LUNCH

QUESADILLAS WITH SALSA, GUACAMOLE AND TORTILLA CHIPS

CORN AND JICAMA SALAD

MARINATED TIJUANA BLACK BEANS

GARBANZO BEAN AND LENTIL SALAD

MEXICAN CHICKEN FAJITAS

TEXAS STYLE BABY BACK RIBS

GRILLED ASSORTED VEGETABLES

JALAPENO BLACK-EYED PEAS

CILANTRO LIME RICE

AUTHENTIC CORNBREAD MUFFINS

PECAN PIE

TEXAS SHEET CAKE

MOCK SANGRIA

COFFEE

FOOD COST

Purchased $263.69
On Hand . . . . $
Subtotal $263.69
Less Credit . . . . $
Total Food Purchased $263.69

LABORATORY ANALYSIS

Total Costs $263.69
Number of Guests 24
Cost/Guest $10.99
    Selling Price at:
    40% $27.48
    35% $31.40
    30% $36.33
Total Sales (Based on 35% food cost) $753.60
Food Purchases $263.69
Total Profit $489.91

	Quantity	Item	Unit	Cost/Unit	Total
1					
2					
3					
4	2	Tomatoes	Each	$0.50	1.00
5	3	Yellow peppers	Each	$1.50	$4.50
6	10	Red peppers	Each	$1.50	$15.00
7	11	Green peppers	Each	$0.50	$5.50
8	2	Purple onions	Each	$0.75	$1.50
9	5	Parsley	Bnch.	$0.50	$2.50
10	3	Oranges	Each	$0.24	$0.72
11	4.5	Corn kernels	Lb.	$1.49	$6.70
12	3	Jicama	Lb.	$1.69	$5.07
13	18	Carrots	Each	$0.10	$1.80
14	3	Cherry tomatoes	Pt.	$1.19	$3.57
15	5	Green onions	Bnch.	$0.13	$0.66
16	2.5	Onions	Lb.	$1.04	$2.60
17	4	Yellow squash	Each	$0.50	$2.00
18	5	Zucchini	Each	$0.60	$3.00
19	10	Garlic	Clove	$0.10	$1.00
20	13	Jalapeno peppers	Each	$0.23	$3.00
21	15	Cilantro	Tbls.	$0.19	$2.85
22	4	Lime	Each	$0.33	$1.32
23	2	Lemon	Each	$0.25	$0.50
24	0.5	Fresh basil	Cup	$3.00	$1.50
25					
26					
27					
28					
29		PRODUCE TOTAL			$67.76

Continued.

	Quantity	Item	Unit	Cost/Unit	Total
1	1	Walnuts	Cup	$2.00	2.00
2	4.5	Olive oil	Cup	$4.00	$18.00
3	1	Red wine vinegar	Cup	$0.58	$0.58
4	4	Cumin	Tbls.	$0.50	$2.00
5	8	Salt	Tsp.	$0.05	$0.40
6	7	Pepper	Tsp.	$0.05	$0.35
7	8	Black beans	Cup	$0.25	$2.00
8	6	Lime juice	Oz.	$0.28	$1.70
9	0.5	Orange juice	Cup	$1.00	$0.50
10	3	Cayenne	Tsp.	$0.40	$1.20
11	12	Lemon juice	Oz.	$0.10	$1.20
12	10	Bay leaves	Each	$0.05	$0.50
13	90	Garbanzo beans	Oz.	$0.06	$5.40
14	1	Chili powder	Oz.	$0.50	$0.50
15	0.5	Seasoned salt	Cup	$2.40	$1.20
16	3	Kraft BBQ Sauce	Cup	$0.63	$1.87
17	3	Ketchup	Cup	$0.56	$1.68
18	1.5	Brown sugar	Cup	$0.50	$0.75
19	1	Dry mustard	Tbls.	$0.28	$0.28
20	1.25	Tabasco	Cup	$0.72	$0.90
21	4	Black-eyed peas	Lb.	$2.19	$8.76
22	20	Beef stock	Cup	$0.33	$6.60
23	12	Pimento	Oz.	$0.32	$3.84
24	2	Oregano	Tsp.	$0.05	$0.10
25	2	Paprika	Tsp.	$0.25	$0.50
26	2.25	Long grain c. rice	Lb.	$1.59	$3.58
27	3	Vegetable oil	Oz.	$0.07	$0.29
28	7	Sugar	Cup	$0.25	$1.75
29	8	Shortening	Oz.	$0.10	$0.80
30	1	Cornmeal	Lb.	$1.79	$1.79
31	2.5	Pastry flour	Lb.	$0.25	$0.63
32	3	Baking powder	Tbls.	$0.10	$0.30
33	1	Maraschino cher.	Cup	$1.49	$1.49
34	3	Corn syrup	Cup	$0.30	$0.90
35	4	Vanilla	Tsp.	$0.25	$1.00
36	4.5	Pecans	Cup	$1.50	$6.75
37	8	Cocoa	Tbls.	$0.33	$2.64
38	1	Baking Soda	Tsp.	$0.10	$0.10
39	2	Powdered sugar	Cup	$0.70	1.40
40	6	Lentils	Cup	$0.70	$4.20
41					
42					
43					
44					
45		DRY STORAGE TOTAL:			$88.98

	Quantity	Item	Unit	Cost/Unit	Total
1	15	Bnls. chicken brst	Halves	$1.00	$15.00
2	6	Baby back ribs	Lb.	$3.99	$24.00
3					
4		MEAT TOTAL:			$39.00
5					
6					
7	6.75	Sour cream	Cup	$1.00	$6.00
8	6	Guacamole	Cup	$1.00	$6.00
9	1	Monterey jack	Cup	$1.00	$1.00
10	4	Cheddar cheese	Cup	$1.00	$4.00
11	27	Milk	Oz.	$0.05	$1.20
12	19	Eggs	Each	$0.10	$1.90
13	6	Butter	Tbls.	$0.10	$0.60
14	0.75	Margarine	Lb.	$1.89	$1.42
15					
16		DAIRY TOTAL:			$22.87
17					
18					
19	10	Corn tortillas	Each	$0.13	$1.30
20	6	Salsa	Cup	$0.50	$3.00
21	30	Flour tortillas	Each	$0.20	$6.00
22	6	Tortilla chips	Bags	$1.49	$8.94
23	168	Sparkling gr. juice	Oz.	$0.13	$22.05
24	3	Raw pie crust	Each	$1.25	$3.75
25					
26		MISCELLANEOUS TOTAL:			$45.08
27					
28					
29					
30					
31					
32		Subtotal:			$106.95

FOOD COST

Continued.

MARKET PURCHASE FORM TOTAL COST

Produce item total: $67.76

Dry storage item total: $88.98

Meat item total: $39.00

Dairy item total: $22.87

Miscellaneous item total: $45.08

ALL ITEM TOTAL: $263.69

	Ingredients	Amount	Unit	Cost/Unit	Total
1	Corn tortillas	10.00	Each	$0.13	$1.30
2	Monterey Jack	1.00	C	$1.00	$1.00
3	Cheddar cheese	1.00	C	$1.00	$1.00
4	Scallions	1.00	C	$0.99	0.99
5	Tomatoes	1.00	C	$0.99	$0.99
6	Jalapeno peppers	0.50	C	$2.00	$1.00
7	Sour cream	6.00	C	$1.00	$6.00
8	Guacamole	6.00	C	$1.00	$6.00
9	Salsa	6.00	C	$0.50	$3.00
10					
11					
12					
13	Total recipe cost:	$21.28			
14					
15	Portion Cost:	$0.89			
16					
17	Date:	3/26/97			
18					
19	Recipe: Quesadillas				
20					
21	Source: D. Bell				

	Ingredients	Amount	Unit	Method
1	Corn tortillas	10.00	Each	Heat griddle to very hot.
2	Monterey Jack	1.00	C	Lay tortilla flat on griddle, sprinkle generously with a portion of all ingredients.
3	Cheddar cheese	1.00	C	
4	Scallions	1.00	C	Fold in half, press and cook each side for 2 minutes.
5	Tomatoes	1.00	C	
6	Jalapeno peppers	0.50	C	When slightly cooler, cut into pie-shaped pieces.
7	Sour cream	6.00	C	
8	Guacamole	6.00	C	Serve with sauces.
9	Salsa	6.00	C	
10				
11				
12	Recipe: Quesadillas			
13				
14	Source: D. Bell			
15				
16	Date: 3/26/97			
17				
18	Yield: 60 pieces			

FOOD COST

Continued.

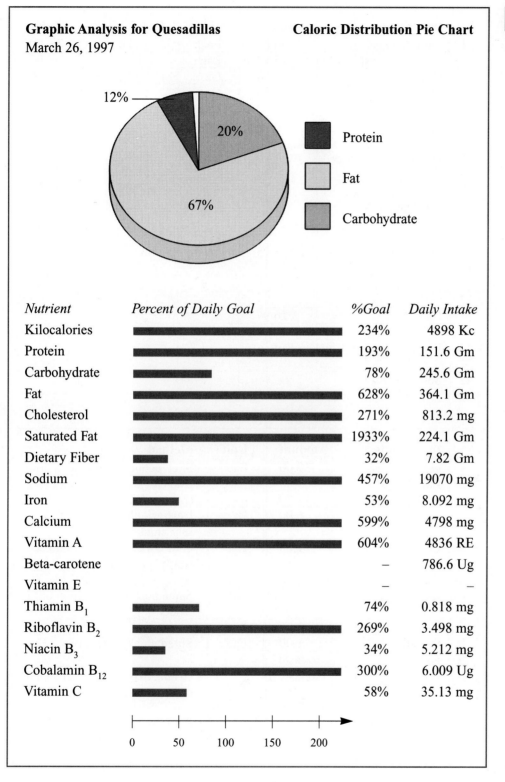

Graphic Analysis for Quesadillas
March 26, 1997

Caloric Distribution Pie Chart

- Protein
- Fat
- Carbohydrate

12% — 20% — 67%

Nutrient	Percent of Daily Goal	%Goal	Daily Intake
Kilocalories		234%	4898 Kc
Protein		193%	151.6 Gm
Carbohydrate		78%	245.6 Gm
Fat		628%	364.1 Gm
Cholesterol		271%	813.2 mg
Saturated Fat		1933%	224.1 Gm
Dietary Fiber		32%	7.82 Gm
Sodium		457%	19070 mg
Iron		53%	8.092 mg
Calcium		599%	4798 mg
Vitamin A		604%	4836 RE
Beta-carotene		–	786.6 Ug
Vitamin E		–	–
Thiamin B_1		74%	0.818 mg
Riboflavin B_2		269%	3.498 mg
Niacin B_3		34%	5.212 mg
Cobalamin B_{12}		300%	6.009 Ug
Vitamin C		58%	35.13 mg

0   50   100   150   200

Continued.

	Ingredients	Amount	Unit	Cost/Unit	Total
1	Flour tortillas	30.00	Each	$0.20	$6.00
2	Chicken breast	15.00	Each	$1.00	$15.00
3	Oil	6.00	Oz.	$0.10	$0.60
4	Cumin	1.00	Oz.	$0.50	$0.50
5	Chili powder	1.00	Oz.	$0.50	$0.50
6	Red peppers	3.00	Each	$1.50	$4.50
7	Green peppers	3.00	Each	$0.50	$1.50
8	Onions	1.00	Each	$0.60	$0.60
9	Salt	to	taste	$0.05	$0.05
10	Pepper	to	taste	$0.05	$0.05
11	Cheddar cheese	3.00	C	$1.25	$3.75
12					
13					
14	Total Recipe Cost:	$33.05			
15					
16	Portion Cost:	$1.38			
17					
18	Date:	3/26/97			
19					
20	Recipe: Mexican Chicken Fajitas				
21					
22	Source: D. Bell				

	Ingredients	Amount	Unit	Method
1	Flour tortillas	30.00	Each	Slice peppers and onions thinly.
2	Bnls. chicken breast	15.00	Each	Rub chicken with oil and spices mixture.
3	Oil	6.00	Oz.	Heat griddle to very hot, sear chicken and cook
4	Cumin	1.00	Oz.	until done. Set aside and keep warm.
5	Chili powder	1.00	Oz.	
6	Red peppers	3.00	Each	Saute peppers and onion until tender.
7	Green peppers	3.00	Each	
8	Onions	1.00	Each	Shred chicken with two forks.
9	Salt	to taste		
10	Pepper	to taste		Arrange fillings in shells and roll up.
11	Cheddar cheese	3.00	C	
12				Put in sprayed hotel pan, heat 10 minutes
13				at 375°F before service.
14				
15	Recipe: Mexican Chicken Fajitas			
16				
17	Source: D. Bell			
18				
19	Date: 3/26/97			
20				
21	Yield: 30 Fajitas			

FOOD COST

Continued.

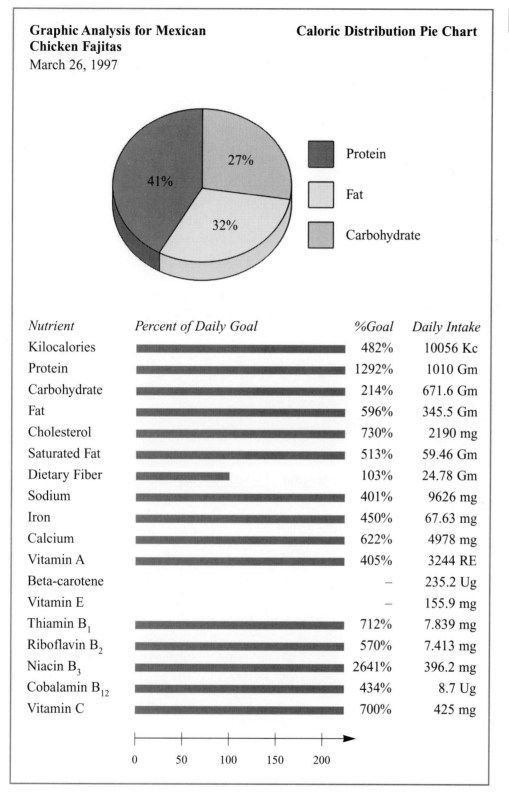

Graphic Analysis for Mexican Chicken Fajitas
March 26, 1997

Caloric Distribution Pie Chart

Pie chart: 27% Protein, 32% Fat, 41% Carbohydrate

Nutrient	Percent of Daily Goal	%Goal	Daily Intake
Kilocalories		482%	10056 Kc
Protein		1292%	1010 Gm
Carbohydrate		214%	671.6 Gm
Fat		596%	345.5 Gm
Cholesterol		730%	2190 mg
Saturated Fat		513%	59.46 Gm
Dietary Fiber		103%	24.78 Gm
Sodium		401%	9626 mg
Iron		450%	67.63 mg
Calcium		622%	4978 mg
Vitamin A		405%	3244 RE
Beta-carotene		–	235.2 Ug
Vitamin E		–	155.9 mg
Thiamin B_1		712%	7.839 mg
Riboflavin B_2		570%	7.413 mg
Niacin B_3		2641%	396.2 mg
Cobalamin B_{12}		434%	8.7 Ug
Vitamin C		700%	425 mg

0   50   100   150   200

	Ingredients	Amount	Unit	Cost/Unit	Total
1	Black-eyed peas	4.00	Lb.	$2.19	$8.76
2	Beef stock	20.00	C	$0.33	$6.60
3	Garlic	8.00	Clove	$0.10	$0.80
4	Jalapenos	10.00	Each	$0.30	$3.00
5	Bay leaf	6.00	Each	$0.05	$0.30
6	Pimentos (diced)	3.00	4 oz. jars	$1.29	$3.87
7	Oregano	2.00	Tsp.	$0.05	$0.10
8	Cumin	2.00	Tsp.	$0.05	$0.10
9	Paprika	2.00	Tsp.	$0.25	$0.50
10	Salt	to	taste	$0.05	$0.05
11	Pepper	to	taste	$0.05	$0.05
12					
13					
14	Total recipe cost:	$24.13			
15					
16	Portion cost:	$1.00			
17					
18	Date:	3/26/97			
19					
20	Recipe: Jalapeno black-eyed peas				
21	Source: Bon Appetit				

	Ingredients	Amount	Unit	Method
1	Black-eyed peas	4.00	Lb.	Cover peas with water (3 inches over top). Soak
2	Beef stock	20.00	C	overnight.
3	Minced garlic	8.00	Clove	
4	Jalapeno peppers	10.00	Each	Drain peas, return to sauce pot. Add stock, onion,
5	Bay leaf	6.00	Each	garlic, chilies, bay leaves, and seasonings. Bring to
6	Pimentos diced	3.00	4oz. jars	a boil. Reduce heat and simmer until peas are tender,
7	Oregano	2.00	Tsp.	stirring often (1.5 hours).
8	Cumin	2.00	Tsp.	
9	Paprika	2.00	Tsp.	Mix pimentos into peas. Season with salt and pepper.
10	Salt	to	taste	
11	Pepper	to	taste	Cover and refrigerate day ahead.
12				
13				Return to boil before service.
14				
15				
16	Recipe: Jalapeno black-eyed peas			
17	Source: Bon Appetit			
18				
19	Date: 3/26/97			
20	Yield: 30 Servings			

FOOD COST

Continued.

Graphic Analysis for Jalapeno Black-eyed Peas
March 26, 1997

Caloric Distribution Pie Chart

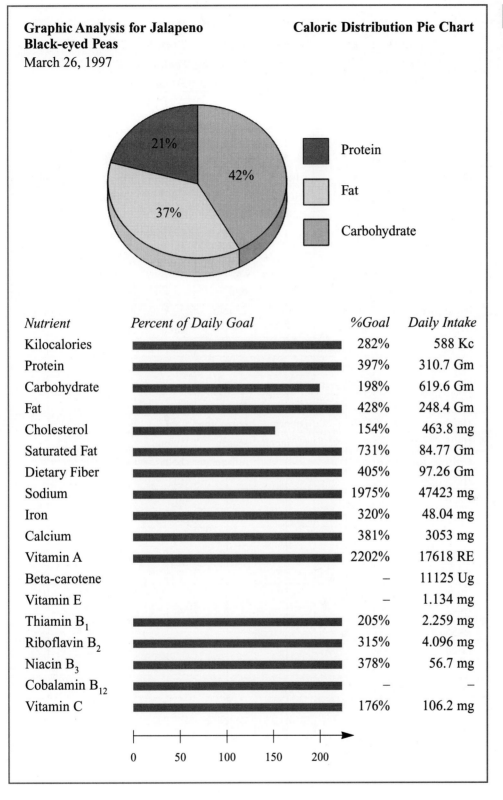

Nutrient	Percent of Daily Goal	%Goal	Daily Intake
Kilocalories		282%	588 Kc
Protein		397%	310.7 Gm
Carbohydrate		198%	619.6 Gm
Fat		428%	248.4 Gm
Cholesterol		154%	463.8 mg
Saturated Fat		731%	84.77 Gm
Dietary Fiber		405%	97.26 Gm
Sodium		1975%	47423 mg
Iron		320%	48.04 mg
Calcium		381%	3053 mg
Vitamin A		2202%	17618 RE
Beta-carotene		–	11125 Ug
Vitamin E		–	1.134 mg
Thiamin B_1		205%	2.259 mg
Riboflavin B_2		315%	4.096 mg
Niacin B_3		378%	56.7 mg
Cobalamin B_{12}		–	–
Vitamin C		176%	106.2 mg

	TEAM 1	TEAM 2	TEAM 3	TEAM 4	TEAM 5	TEAM 6	TEAM 7
	Quesa.	*Jicama*	*Bl. Bean*	*Garb. Bn*	*Fajitas*	*Ribs*	*Sauce*
08:30	Set up	Set up	Set up	Set up	Set up	Set up	Set up
08:35							
08:40							
08:45							
08:50	↓	↓	↓	↓	↓	↓	↓
08:55	Season chix	Chop	Chop	Dice carrots	Slice veg.	Wash	Blend
09:00	Heat	Jicama,	All Veg.	Combine	Prepare	Drain	All
09:05	Griddle.	Cilantro.	Boil beans	Water	Chix	Season	Ingredients
09:10	↓			Carrot	Grill chix	ribs.	reserve
09:15	Lay out			lentils		slow	
09:20	tortillas			bay leaf.		cook	
09:25	fill with	↓		boil			
09:30	ingredients	combine		25 min.	↓		
09:35		all			shred		
09:40		ingredients	↓				
09:45		reserve	combine	↓	↓		
09:50	↓	refrigerate	all ingred.	cool	saute veg.		
09:55	spray cook		salt	mix			
10:00	surface		pepper	remaining	↓		
10:05	with Pam.		refrigerate	season	lay out		
10:10	fold shells			refrigerate	shells		
10:15	in half				fill		
10:20	begin				roll		
10:25	cooking				pan up		
10:30					refrigerate		
10:35							
10:40							
10:45						↓	
10:50						check	
10:55						continue	
11:00	↓						
11:05	cool						
11:10	slightly						
11:15	slice hold						
11:20							
11:25							
11:30					↓	↓	
11:35					reheat	sauce	
11:40					for	continue	
11:45					service		
11:50	↓						
11:55	serve to	↓	↓	↓	↓	↓	↓
12:00	table	serve	serve	serve	serve	serve	serve

EMPLOYEE SCHEDULING

	TEAM 1	TEAM 2	TEAM 3	TEAM 4	TEAM 5	TEAM 6	TEAM 7
	Gr. Veg.	*Jal. Peas*	*Rice*	*Corn Br.*	*Sangria*	*Pie*	*Cake*
08:30	Set up	Set up	Set up	Set up	Set up	Set up	Set up
08:35							
08:40							
08:45	↓	↓	↓	↓	↓	↓	↓
08:50	Mince basil	Follow	Heat pan	Preheat	Slice	Mix first	Boil first
08:55	Mix with	recipe	add oil.	425 oven	fruit	five	three
09:00	oil, salt	cook.	onion	cream	reserve	ingredients	ingredients
09:05	pepper		sweat.	ingredients		add	mix flour,
09:10	slice veg.		add	add eggs		pecans	sugar,
09:15	brush		garlic.	add milk		pour into	salt
09:20	on oil		add rice.	cornmeal		pastry	baking soda
09:25			water,	sift dry		shells	combine
09:30	↓		S&P	ingredients		bake	all
09:35	heat		cook	in recipe			add eggs
09:40	grill		20-25 min.	combine			sour cream
09:45				all.			mix well
09:50				fill			pour in pan
09:55				tins			bake
10:00	↓			bake			
10:05	grill		↓				
10:10	al dente		add line				
10:15	hold	↓	juice				↓
10:20		add	and zest.	↓			cool
10:25		pimentos	hold hot.	hold.			
10:30		season			↓	↓	
10:35		hold, hot			add juice	cool	
10:40					hold		
10:45							
10:50							
10:55							↓
11:00							frost
11:05							cut
11:10							
11:15							
11:20							
11:25							
11:30	↓						
11:35	reheat						
11:40					↓		
11:45					add ice	↓	
11:50					and	cut	
11:55	↓	↓	↓	↓	cherries	and	↓
12:00	serve	serve	serve	serve	serve	serve	serve

ROOM CONFIGURATION

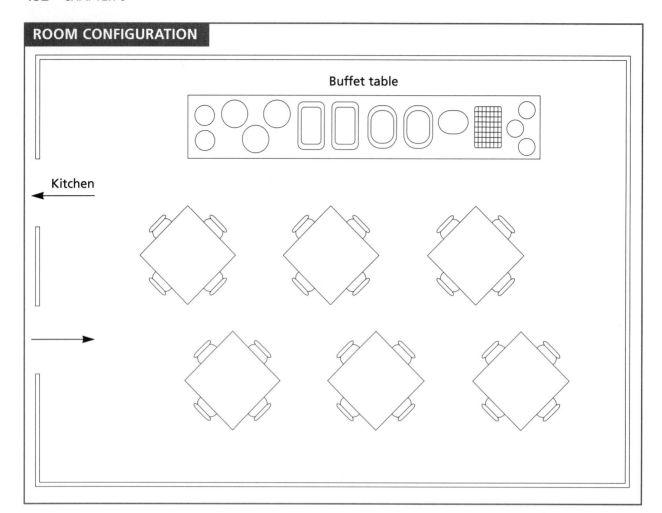

Buffet table

Kitchen

TABLETOP DESIGN

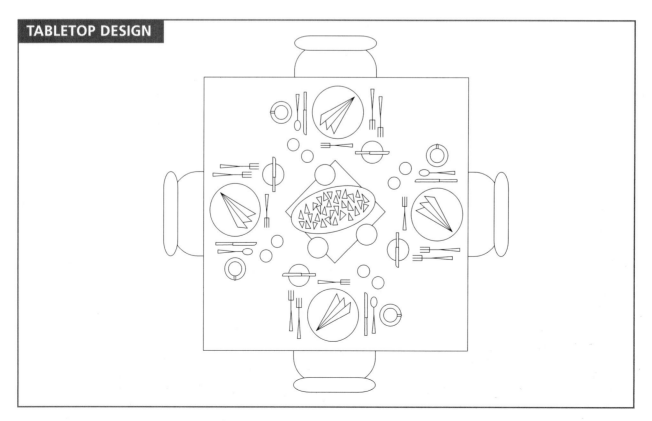

INVENTORY LIST

Dinner Plates	30
Salad Plates	60
B&B Plates	30
Coffee Saucer	30
Coffee Cups	30
Creamer	6
Sugar Bowls	6
Butter Plate	6
Water Glass	30
Wine Glass	30
Dinner Knife	30
B&B Knife	60
Dinner Fork	30
Salad Fork	30
Fish Fork	
Dessert Fork	30
Soup Spoon	
Tea Spoon	30
Dessert Spoon	
Salt & Pepper Shakers	6
Soup Bowls	
Monkey Dish	18
Appetizer Plates	30
Soup Cups	
Candle Holders	
Votives	
Chafing Dishes	4
Serving Spoons	8
Serving Forks	8
Tongs	4
Pie Server	4
Pie Stands	4
Elevation Boxes	2
Vases	
Baskets	8
Pitchers	4

EVENT/ROOM SPECIFICATIONS

Linen Order:

Tablecloths: 6-50" White Cotton, 3-120" White Cotton

Napkins: 40 White, 10 Red

Musical Selections: Herb Alpert and the Tijuana Brass, Gloria Estefan

Decorations: Southwestern Motif

Items provided by the Foods II class.

You're right on target . . .

if you're thinking

Hospitality Management

Is there a class where I can learn how to cook?

Call Linda for information at ext. 6736

Happy Holidays

from the

HOSPITALITY DEPARTMENT

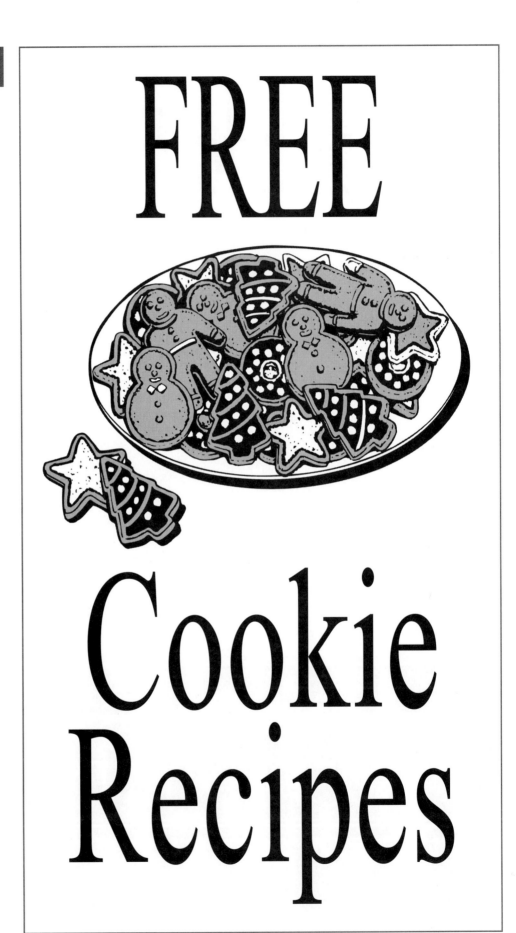

FREE

Cookie Recipes

COOKIES FOR CHRISTMAS

Orange Cookies

Makes about 3 dozen

¾ cup confectioners' sugar

⅔ cup unsalted butter, softened

2 tablespoons grated orange zest

¼ cup fresh orange juice

1¾ cup all-purpose flour

Pinch of salt

Colored crystal sugar, Sugar Glaze, or Piping Icing for decoration

1. In a large mixer bowl, beat the confectioners' sugar and butter until smooth and fluffy, 3 to 4 minutes. Add the orange zest and juice and beat until smooth.

2. Gradually add the flour and salt, beating until just smooth. Cover with plastic wrap and refrigerate until the dough is firm, at least 1 hour.

3. Preheat the oven to 325°F. On a lightly floured surface, roll out one-quarter of the dough ⅛ inch thick. Cut out the dough with cookie cutters and place 1 inch apart on ungreased cookie sheets.

4. Bake the cookies for 25 minutes, or until lightly golden around the edges. To decorate, sprinkle the cookies with crystal sugar while still warm and then transfer to a rack to cool. Or, let the cookies cool and then decorate with Sugar Glaze or Piping Icing. Store in layers, separated by sheets of waxed paper, in an airtight tin.

Sugar Glaze

Enough for 4 to 5 dozen cookies

3 tablespoons milk

½ teaspoon vanilla extract

3½ cups (1 lb. box) confectioners' sugar

Food coloring

1. In a medium bowl, combine the milk and vanilla. Slowly stir in the sugar, beating constantly until the glaze becomes thick and creamy. The more this glaze is beaten, the shinier it becomes.

2. Divide the glaze among several small bowls. Stir a few drops of the desired food coloring into each bowl. If the glaze becomes too thin, stir in a few teaspoons of confectioners' sugar. Spread on cooled cookies with a broad flat knife.

Note: To prevent the glaze in the bowls from forming a crust while decorating, keep covered with a dampened cloth.

Cottage Butter Cookies.

Makes about 4 dozen

1 cup (2 sticks) unsalted butter, softened

⅔ cup sugar

1 teaspoon vanilla extract

½ teaspoon lemon extract

1 egg

2½ cups all-purpose flour

1 teaspoon baking powder

Colored crystal sugar, Sugar Glaze or Piping Icing for decoration

1. In a large mixer bowl, beat the butter and sugar until smooth and fluffy, 3 to 4 minutes. Add the vanilla and lemon extracts and the egg; beat until smooth and light, 2 to 3 minutes.

2. Add 1¼ cups of the flour and ½ teaspoon of the baking powder. Beat until just smooth; add the remaining 1½ cups flour and ½ teaspoon baking powder and mix to combine. Cover the dough with plastic wrap and refrigerate until firm, at least 1 hour.

3. Preheat the oven to 325°F. On a lightly floured surface, roll out one-quarter of the dough ⅛ inch thick. Cut the dough out with decorative cookie cutters and place 1 inch apart on ungreased cookie sheets.

4. Bake the cookies for 20 minutes, or until lightly golden around the edges. To decorate, sprinkle the cookies with crystal sugar while still warm and then transfer to a rack to cool. Or, let the cookies cool and then decorate with Sugar Glaze or Piping Icing. Store in layers, separated by sheets of waxed paper, in an airtight tin.

Piping Icing

Makes about 2 cups

1 egg white, lightly beaten

2 to 3 cups confectioners' sugar, sifted

Several drops of fresh lemon juice

Food coloring

1. Place the egg white in a medium bowl. Gradually stir in the sugar and lemon juice until the mixture is stiff.

2. Divide the sugar mixture among several small bowls. Stir a few drops of the desired food coloring into each bowl. If the icing becomes too thin, stir in a few teaspoons of sifted confectioners' sugar. Pipe onto cooled cookies. Note: To prevent the icing from forming a crust while decorating, keep icing in the bowls covered with a dampened cloth.

RECIPES
for a
Romantic Dinner

SAINT PATRICK'S DAY

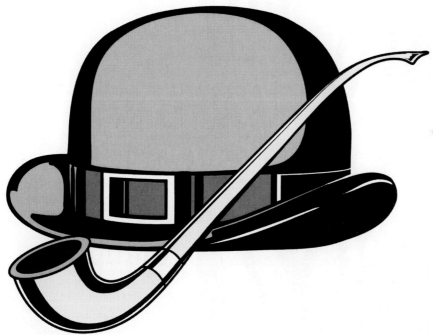

PARTY!

Thinking of Spring

Boyce
Campus

Hospitality
Management

WORKS IN
PROGRESS

Continued.

FREE

Spring Recipes

SPRING BRUNCH

Belgian Endive and Snow Pea Salad

8 Servings

3 tablespoons red wine vinegar

2 tablespoons Dijon mustard

½ teaspoon salt

½ cup plus 1 tablespoon olive oil

3 tablespoons chopped shallots

freshly ground pepper

1 pound snow peas, ends trimmed diagonally, strings removed

6 heads Belgian endive

1. Whisk vinegar, mustard, and salt in small bowl. Gradually whisk in oil. Mix in shallots. Season with pepper. *(Can be prepared ahead. Let stand at room temperature. Whisk before using.)*

2. Blanch snow peas in large pot of boiling salted water 30 seconds. Drain. Refresh under cold water. Drain and pat dry. Transfer to large bowl.

3. Peel off outer leaves from Belgian endive and arrange in spoke fashion on large platter. Cut remaining endive into julienne. Add to snow peas. Add enough dressing to season to taste and toss well.

4. Mound salad in center of endive-lined platter and serve.

Eggs Baked with Leeks and Tarragon

8 Servings

4 tablespoons (½ stick) unsalted butter

3 large leeks (white and pale green parts only), coarsely chopped

1½ cups grated Gruyère cheese (about 6 oz.)

½ cup freshly grated Parmesan cheese (about 2 oz.)

8 large eggs

2 cups whipping cream

2 tablespoons plus 2 teaspoons chopped fresh tarragon or 1½ teaspoons dried, crumbled tarragon

½ teaspoon salt

¼ teaspoon freshly ground pepper

fresh tarragon sprigs

1. Preheat oven to 375°F. Butter 9x13-inch glass baking dish with 1 tablespoon butter.

2. Melt remaining 3 tablespoons butter in heavy large skillet over medium-high heat. Add leeks and sauté until tender, about 5 minutes. Spread in bottom of prepared dish.

3. Combine cheeses in bowl. Spread all but ½ cup cheese over leeks in dish.

4. Whisk eggs, cream, chopped tarragon, salt, and pepper in large bowl to blend. Pour into dish.

5. Bake casserole until top is golden brown and center is set, about 30 minutes.

6. Sprinkle remaining ½ cup cheese over the top. Bake until cheese melts, about 5 more minutes. Garnish with tarragon sprigs and serve.

Crisp Biscuits with Ham and Orange Marmalade

Makes about 24

2 cups all-purpose flour

1 tablespoon sugar

2 teaspoons baking powder

½ teaspoon baking soda

½ teaspoon salt

¼ cup solid vegetable shortening, chilled and cut into small pieces

2 tablespoons (1/4 stick) unsalted butter, chilled and cut into small pieces

¾ cup buttermilk

1 egg yolk

3 tablespoons unsalted butter, melted

½ pound cooked ham (e.g., Honey-Baked), sliced thin

¼ cup orange marmalade

1. Preheat oven to 425°F. Mix first 5 ingredients in large bowl. Add shortening and chilled butter and cut in until mixture resembles coarse meal.

2. Make well in center. Add 1/2 cup buttermilk and egg yolk to well and stir until dough begins to come together, adding more buttermilk by tablespoons as necessary to form soft dough.

3. Gather dough into ball. Turn dough out onto lightly floured surface and gently knead 30 seconds.

4. Roll dough out to 3/8-inch thick round. Cut into 2-inch rounds using cookie cutter. Gather scraps and reroll. Cut out additional rounds.

5. Transfer to 2 heavy, large cookie sheets. Bake until tops are golden brown and bottoms are crisp, about 15 minutes.

6. Cool biscuits slightly. Split in half horizontally. Brush insides with melted butter. Arrange ham over bottom halves, trimming to fit. Spread with marmalade. Assemble and serve.

Hazelnut Butter Cookies

Makes about 3 dozen

2 cups all-purpose flour

¼ teaspoon baking soda

pinch of salt

1 cup (2 sticks) unsalted butter, room temperature

1 cup hazelnuts, toasted, husked, coarsely ground

½ cup sugar

1 egg yolk

2½ teaspoons vanilla extract

2 cups powdered sugar

1. Position rack in center of oven and preheat to 350°F.

2. Combine flour, baking soda, and salt in large bowl. Add butter and cut in until mixture resembles coarse meal. Add nuts, ½ cup sugar, egg yolk, and vanilla, and mix until smooth dough forms.

3. Shape dough into 1-inch balls. Place on heavy large cookie sheets, spacing evenly. Press balls with back of fork in crisscross pattern to form ¼-inch thick cookies.

4. Bake cookies until tops begin to color and bottoms are pale golden brown, about 20 minutes.

5. Spread 1 cup powdered sugar in large shallow dish. Transfer cookies to dish. Spoon remaining powdered sugar over cookies. Roll cookies in powdered sugar in dish. Cool.

COMMUNITY
COLLEGE OF
ALLEGHENY
COUNTY

Office of the Registrar
800 Allegheny Avenue
Pittsburgh, PA 15233-1895
(412)237-3185

Academic Transcript

```
                    PHI THETA KAPPA
CIPRIANI DONNA M.    CAMPUS: BOYCE    DATE: 06/03/98    PAGE 1 OF 1
                                CRS.    Q.P.    Q.P.A.
                    CUM AVG     767     265     1196    CURRENT MAJOR:

SP COURSE CMP COURSE                    SP  COURSE    CMP COURSE
CODE NUMBER      TITLE       CR GR  QP  CODE NO.      TITLE      CR GR
QP

FALL SEMESTER 1996-97
DVS103    A    ADV COL RD/ST SK 3 A   12
ENG101    A    ENGLISH COMP 1     3 B    9
HOA101    A    HOSPITALITY MGT    3 A   12
HOA102    A    FOOD SERVICE 1     3 A   12
MAT080    A    ARITHMETIC FUND    4 A   16
TOTALS        QPA 3.81  16  61

SPRING SEMESTER 1996-97
CIS100 A    INTRO COMPUTERS    3 A   12
ENG102 A    ENGLISH COMP 2     3 A   12
HOA104 A    FOOD/BEV SERV      3 A   12
HOA105 A    SUPV & TRAINING    3 A   12
HOA112 A    FOOD SERVICE 2     3 A   12
TOTALS      QPA 4.00  15  60

2ND SUMMER SESSION 1997
ACC101 A    ACCOUNT PRIN 1     3 A   12
ECO102 A    PRIN MACROECONMC   3 A   12
TOTALS      QPA 4.00   6  24

FALL SEMESTER 1997-98
BUS103 A    PRIN MANAGEMENT    3 A   12
BUS251 A    BUSINESS LAW 1     3 A   12
HOA201 A    HOTL/MO OFF PRO    3 A   12
HOA203 A    HTL-MTL SLS/PROM   3 A   12
HOA303 A    IND STD HOSP ADM   3 A   12
SPH101 A    ORAL COMM          3 A   12
TOTALS      QPA 4.00  18  72

SPRING SEMESTER 1997-98
BIO117 A    INTRO NUTRITION    3 A   12
BUS104 A    PRIN OF MARKETNG   3 A   12
HOA110 A    HSPTLTY CTRL SYS   3 A   12
HOA205 A    HOSP MGMT PRACTM   3 A   12
TOTALS      QPA 4.00  12  48

CREDIT BY EXAMINATION
04-97  BUSINESS MATH      3 P   BUS120

DEG    DATE    CMP MAJOR         QPA    HONORS
CRT 05/09/98   A   FOOD SERVICE  3.95   HSH
AS  05/09/98   A   HOTEL MOTEL   3.95   HSH           ACADEMIC AFFAIRS
```

The Community College of Allegheny County (CCAC) has four campuses and a College Administrative Office. Each campus is coded on this transcript, and this code (B-Allegheny, A-Boyce, D-North, C-South) appears immediately preceding the course title.

This transcript is an unabridged academic record of any course in which the student was properly registered.

ACCREDITATION

The Community College of Allegheny County is accredited by the Middle States Association of Colleges as a degree granting institution. Certain individual programs are recognized by various professional accrediting agencies in their respective fields. The College awards the AA, AS, and AAS degrees, and certification in selected programs. In the past, the College also awarded diplomas. This award is no longer issued.

ACADEMIC CALENDAR AND UNIT OF CREDIT

A semester has 15 weeks of instruction, excluding final exams. An academic year starts on July 1, and ends the following year on June 30th. The summer classes are scheduled during a variety of summer sessions. Each session contains the equivalent of 15 weeks of instruction. A Unit of credit is equated to 50 minutes of instruction for 15 class meetings.

COURSE NUMBERING SYSTEM

The College has used two numbering systems. The first numbering system contained five numbers (11101 English 1). The current number consists of a three letter alpha department plus three numeric numbers (ENG101, English 1). The "11" and the "ENG" represent the academic department. The "101" represents the level of the course. One hundred is first year and two hundred is second year.

Courses numbered three hundred and higher are specialty courses and generally do not transfer. Courses with a number below 100 are considered remedial and do not count toward requirements for an AA or AS degree.

GRADES AND QUALITY POINTS

Value grades:

A student's evaluation in course is indicated by one of the following grades. They carry a point value, and are used in calculating the student's quality point average (QPA).

A	Superior	4 points
B	Above Average	3 points
C	Average	2 points
D	Below Average	1 point
F	Failing	0 points

The QPA is determined by dividing the number of quality points received by the number of credits for the value grades of the same courses.

The following grades and codes are not part of the QPA calculation.

Non-value Grades:	Special Codes:
I Incomplete	• Repeat
L Audit	NG Not Used for Graduation
N Non-Attending	AF Academic Forgiveness/
P Pass	Not Used for Graduation
W Withdrawal	
X No Grade Received by Instructor	

REPEATED COURSES

Students may repeat courses in which they received a "D" or "F" grade. The prior grade will be removed from the calculation of the

quality point average. It will remain on the student's grade record, but coded with an (*) asterisk. The most recent grade will be used in the calculation of the quality point average. If the most recent grade was a non-value grade, it will remain on the student's grade record, but it will not replace the prior value grade in the calculation of the QPA.

COURSES OFFERED UNDER SPECIAL CONTRACTS/AGREEMENTS

If a student is participating in a special contracted program through another college or university, the courses will appear on this transcript as identified by the following course numbers:

Pittsburgh Council on Higher Education (PCHE)
Course Number - PCH99X
The last digit of the number will reflect the number of credits.

The name of the school is coded as the first letter preceding the course title. The codes and the school names are listed below.

The course title reflects the other school's course name.

R	LaRoche College
S	Pittsburgh Theological Seminary
T	Duquesne University
U	Robert Morris College
V	Point Park College
W	University of Pittsburgh
X	Carnegie-Mellon University
Y	Chatham College
Z	Carlow College

Indiana University of Pennsylvania (IUP)

The course number will always begin with a number "1", followed by two alpha department codes, and three numeric course numbers. These course numbers belong to IUP, are offered on the CCAC campus to only CCAC students, and are not listed in the CCAC catalog. Course descriptions are available from IUP.

HONORS NOTATION

Over the years, the College has awarded academic honors to students. These awards are listed on the transcript as one the of the following codes.

H	Honors
HH	High Honors
HSH	Highest Honors
PTK	Phi Theta Kappa

COURSE/GRADE CHANGES

When any change is made to a specific course/grade record, a change code is listed next to the course number. If there is a need to know why the change was made, contact the Office of the Registrar at (412)237-3185.

RELEASE OF TRANSCRIPT

This transcript is released only with the written consent of the student. As an official CCAC record, this transcript should not be awarded to a third party outside the receiving institution. The student should request another official transcript from CCAC.

TRANSCRIPT FEE

There is no charge for and official transcript from the Community College of Allegheny County, and there is no limit to the number requested.

TO TEST FOR AUTHENTICITY: The face of this document has a blue background and the name of the institution appears in small print. Apply fresh liquid bleach to the sample background printed below. If authentic, the paper will turn brown.

COMMUNITY COLLEGE OF ALLEGHENY COUNTY COMMUNITY COLLEGE OF ALLEGHENY COUNTY COMMUNITY COLLEGE OF ALLEGHENY COUNTY COMMUNITY COLLEGE OF ALLEGHENY COUNTY COMMUNITY COLLEGE OF ALLEGHENY COUNTY COMMUNITY COLLEGE OF ALLEGHENY COUNTY COMMUNITY COLLEGE OF ALLEGHENY COUNTY COMMUNITY COLLEGE OF

ADDITIONAL TEST: When photocopied, the word Copy appears prominently across the face of the entire document. ALTERNATION OR FORGERY OF THIS DOCUMENT MAY BE A CRIMINAL OFFENSE! A black and white document is not an original and should not be accepted as an official institutional document. This transcript cannot be released to a third party without the written consent of the student. This is in accordance with the Family Educational Rights and Privacy Act of 1974. If you have questions about this document, please contact our office at (412)237-3185.

TRAINING

HOA101 Introduction To Hospitality Management

3 credits/3 class hours

A study of the history, organization, problems, opportunities, and possible future trends of the hotel—motel and food service industries. The basic functions, procedures, and responsibilities of management are explained.

HOA102 Food Service 1

3 credits/1 lecture and 3 laboratory hours

A study of the fundamentals of food preparation, service procedures, sanitation, and safety practices of the food service business. Controls and management of function are also discussed.

HOA103 Hotel–Motel Housekeeping

3 credits/3 class hours

A study of the organization and functions of the housekeeping departments of hotel and motel establishments. Selections and care of supplies and furnishings as well as practical problems of housekeeping are considered. Emphasis is placed on safety, sanitation, and preventive maintenance.

HOA104 Food and Beverage Service

3 credits/3 class hours

A course in types of dining service appropriate for coffee shops, dining rooms, banquets, and buffets. Included are liquor laws and the service of legal beverages.

HOA105 Supervision and Training

3 credits/3 class hours

A course in the techniques involved in hiring, orienting, training, supervising, and evaluating employees in hotels and food service operations. The use of work simplification as a method of increasing efficiency in management is discussed.

HOA112 Food Service 2

3 credits/1 lecture and 3 laboratory hours
Prerequisite: HOA102 and HOA202

A study of developing standardized recipes and computing food and labor costs. Attention is given to the use and care of small and large kitchen equipment. Experience in planning, preparation, and service is provided in the campus food service laboratory.

HOSPITALITY MANAGEMENT ASSOCIATE DEGREE REQUIREMENTS

Major Core Courses		Credits
HOA101	Intro. to Hospitality Management	3
HOA102	Food Service 1	3
HOA104	Food and Beverage Service	3
HOA105	Supervision and Training	3
HOA202	Purchasing Procedures	3
HOA205	Hospitality Management Practicum	3

Specified Electives		
ACC101	Accounting Principles 1	3
BUS103	Principles of Management	3
OAS100	Keyboarding or	
OAS111	Typing 1	3

General Education		
ENG101	English Composition 1	3
ENG102	English Composition 2	3
BUS120	Business Mathematics or	
	Mathematics Elective	3–4
————	Science Elective	3–4
————	Social Science Elective	3
SPH101	Oral Communications	3

Unspecified Electives		
	Electives (2)	6

Hotel-Motel Management Option		
HOA103	Hotel–Motel Housekeeping	3
HOA201	Hotel–Motel Front Office Procedures	3
HOA203	Hotel–Motel Sales and Promotion	3

OR

Food Service Management Option		
HOA112	Food Service 2	3
HOA115	Menu Design	3
BUS250	Business Law 1	3

Minimum Credits to Graduate	60–62

The Pennsylvania Commission for Community Colleges

proudly recognizes the academic achievements of the

1997–98

ALL-PENNSYLVANIA ACADEMIC TEAM

and honors

Donna M. Cipriani

for outstanding performance at

COMMUNITY COLLEGE OF ALLEGHENY COUNTY

(BOYCE CAMPUS)

Frederick W. Capshaw

Dr. Frederick Capshaw, President
Pennsylvania Commission for Community Colleges

Presented at Harrisburg
April 6, 1998

THE COMMUNITY COLLEGE OF ALLEGHENY COUNTY

issues this

DEAN'S LIST CERTIFICATE

to

Donna M. Cipriani

in recognition of high scholastic achievement at the Community College of Allegheny County during the 1996–97 Academic Year.

James C. Holmberg

James C. Holmberg, Ph.D.
Vice President of Academic Affairs

Continued.   AWARDS

THE COMMUNITY COLLEGE OF ALLEGHENY COUNTY

issues this

DEAN'S LIST CERTIFICATE

to

Donna M. Cipriani

in recognition of high scholastic achievement at the Community College of Allegheny County
during the Fall 1997 Semester.

James C. Holmberg

James C. Holmberg, Ph.D.
Vice President of Academic Affairs

THE COMMUNITY COLLEGE OF ALLEGHENY COUNTY

issues this

DEAN'S LIST CERTIFICATE

to

Donna M. Cipriani

in recognition of high scholastic achievement at the Community College of Allegheny County
during the Spring 1998 Semester.

James C. Holmberg

James C. Holmberg, Ph.D.
Vice President of Academic Affairs

PHI THETA KAPPA

International Honor Society of the Two-Year College
SINCE 1918

Center for Excellence
Mississippi Education & Research Center
1625 Eastover Drive
Jackson, MS 39211-6431

Headquarters
Phone: 601.957.2241
Toll-free: 800.946.9995
Fax: 601.957.2625

February 20, 1997

Donna Cipriani
804 Jones Drive
Pittsburgh, PA 15235

Dear Donna,

Congratulations upon your outstanding achievement which earned you nomination for the 1998 All-USA Academic Team for Community and Junior Colleges.

The academic standard and commitment to community service exemplified by you during your college enrollment is commendable. Unfortunately, due to the limited number of positions on the First, Second, and Third Academic Teams, your nomination was not selected for recognition in *USA Today*. Approximately 1,300 nominations were received this year, each of which represented the top 99th percentile of their sponsoring two-year institution.

For your participation in the 1998 All-USA Academic Team competition, we are pleased to present you with a certificate of recognition. This certificate will be mailed directly to your college president for his or her signature in early March.

We appreciate you and your college submitting a nomination for the 1998 All-USA Academic Team. Through your participation, you have become part of the movement to showcase the outstanding students enrolled in our two-year colleges.

We wish you the very best with your future academic endeavors.

Sincerely,

Rod A. Risley

Rod A. Risley
Executive Director

C.C.A.C. BOYCE CAMPUS

Phi Theta Kappa

proudly awards

Donna M. Cipriani

this Certificate of Membership
Given this 7th day of May, 1998

Richard P. Betters
Vice-President/Executive Dean

Charley L. Marton
Dean of STudents

Frank Kaufman
Director of Student Life

Who's Who Among Students
in American Junior Colleges

3200 Rice Rd., NE / P.O. Box 2029 / Tuscaloosa, Alabama 35043
205/349-2990 / 1-800-633-5953

March 3, 1998

Donna Cipriani
804 Jones Drive
Pittsburgh, PA 15235

Dear Ms. Cipriani:

I am privileged to inform you that you are one of 119 students nominated by Community
College of Allegheny County for inclusion in the 1998 edition of Who's Who Among Students
in American Junior Colleges.

A recognized institution of the American academic community, the Who's Who award is
conferred annually upon outstanding student leaders. Over the past 32 years, more than 1,800
junior college have adopted this program as part of their annual campus honors. Selections are
made by campus nominating committees and are based on decidedly above average academic
standing, community service, leadership ability and potential for continued success.

As documentary evidence and recognition of the honor, a certificate will be presented to
you by your college later this year. And, as a lifetime Who's Who member, you are eligible to
use the Reference Service maintained for the exclusive assistance of nominees seeking post-
graduate employment, fellowships or admission to the various voluntary service organizations.
There is never any charge for this service.

Your personal biographical questionnaire is enclosed along with a brochure describing the
Who's Who program. Please complete it carefully and return it by 04/08/98. Your biographical
sketch will be prepared from the information you provide.

Since you will be recognized in the 32nd annual edition of Who's Who Among Students
in American Junior Colleges, you probably would like a personal copy to commemorate your
selection. I have, therefore, placed a tentative order in your name. Please confirm this reservation when you return your Student Profile Questionnaire.

On behalf of the Who's Who program, I would like to congratulate you on your outstanding work and on receiving this highly coveted award. We look forward to presenting your
accomplishments in the 1998 edition of Who's Who Among Students in American Junior
Colleges.

20013-17-0-98

Sincerely,

H. Pettus Randall

H. Pettus Randall
Director

HPR/laz

Who's Who

AMONG STUDENTS IN

American Junior Colleges

This is to certify that

Donna M. Cipriani

has been elected to Who's Who Among Students in
American Junior Colleges in recognition of outstanding merit
and accomplishment as a student at

Community College of Allegheny County

1997–98

H. Freeling Randell
Director

RETURN TO THE ACADEMY BY APRIL 20, 1998

USAA
ALL-AMERICAN SCHOLAR

Collegiate Program   *United States Achievement Academy*

AC MS PACOM CMON 10968 0054

Ms Donna M Cipriani and Parents

Dear Donna M,

You have been officially nominated to receive the All-American Scholar Collegiate Award by Dr Charles P Bostaph.

You may take pride in your nomination as it constitutes the recognition of your outstanding work and academic achievements during your college career. To honor your accomplishments, the United States Achievement Academy will publish your biography in the All-American Scholar Collegiate Directory, a publication which honors academically outstanding college students nationwide.

Of equal importance to you is the fact that, by accepting your award, you become a candidate for All-American Scholar Scholarships. The Scholarship Committee will award these grants each year. Only award winners such as you, whose names and biographies appear in the Directory, are invited to apply.

To be certain that your biography appears, please complete and return the attached All-American Scholar biography form. Since we cannot publish your biography unless we have it before the deadline, we urge you to return you form before April 20, 1998.

Phi Theta Kappa

this is to certify that

Donna M. Cipriani

has complied with all the requirements for and has been inducted into the

Phi Theta Kappa Society

International Scholastic Order of the Two-Year College
In witness of which we have caused the great seal of this Society to be
hereto affixed and inscribed our signatures.

Rod A. Rigley

Executive Director

May 17, 1997

Date

L. Gail Bracken

Chapter Advisor

Sigma Omicron

Chapter

Continued. AWARDS

WORD
FM 101.5 PITTSBURGH

March 5, 1998

Joanne Martin
Assistant to the Executive Dean   Donna Cipriani
Community College of Allegheny County   804 Jones Drive
Pittsburgh, PA 15222   Pittsburgh, PA 15235

Dear Joanne, Donna, Staff & Students,

Now that the last of the cake crumbs have been cleared, it is with immense gratitude that we acknowledge your support of the 1998 Great Cake Auction. Your participation made the event a huge success for the public and most especially, the Make-A-Wish Foundation of Western Pennsylvania.

Thanks for all that you did with the press conference cake decorating and the "People's Choice" Awards! Everything was first rate!

You'll be happy to know that nearly $16,000 was raised at the event, and that does not include what was raised by the Western Pennsylvania Bakers' Association from public donations for a slice of the 2000+ piece Make-A-Wish cake!

The success of the auction means that five children will get their favorite wish . . . whether it's a computer, a trip to Disney World or whatever else their childhood hearts and minds could hope for!

We look forward to the 2nd annual event and we look forward to working with you again! Thanks so very, very much!

Best Ever,

Norma Rachel Dent

Norma Rachel Dent
Coordinator
1998 Great Cake Auction

(412) 937-1500 (Bus.) • (412) 937-1576 (Fax)
Parkway Center, Suite 625, Pittsburgh, PA 15220

Community College
of Allegheny County

BOYCE CAMPUS
595 Beatty Road
Monroeville, PA 15146-1395
1 (724) 371-8651

www.ccac.edu

To Whom it May Concern:

This letter is written on behalf of Donna M. Cipriani, a student at the Community College of Allegheny County, Boyce Campus, who is scheduled to graduate in May of 1998 with an associate's degree in Hotel/Motel Management. Donna is an exceptional student both in her academic pursuits and in her leadership and outstanding service projects. Some of the many projects she has been involved in this academic year include the Adopt-A-Family service project, Adopt-A-Highway service project, tutoring students, and the Angel Tree service project to benefit needy children. What is so outstanding about Donna participating in and leading these as well as many other projects is that she was enrolled for 18 credits each semester and maintains a 3.92 Q.P.A.

Donna is an intelligent, confident, pleasant and hardworking student. She impressed me as an individual with ability, very intent on doing well in whatever she has to do.

An outstanding characteristic that Donna possesses, one which manifests itself in the classroom and in her personal life, is the warmth of her personality and her ability to work with other people. Her performance at Boyce Campus, both as a student leader and as a student, has been painstaking and accurate, always proficient work of fine quality.

I am pleased to recommend Donna Cipriani to you.

Sincerely,

Charles J. Martoni

Charles J. Martoni, Ph.D.
Dean of Students
CJM/jt

BOYCE CAMPUS
595 Beatty Road
Monroeville, PA 15146-1395
1 (724) 371-8651

www.ccac.edu

To Whom it May Concern:

It is indeed a pleasure to offer my recommendation of Donna Cipriani. Donna has been a student of the Community College of Allegheny County, Boyce Campus' Hotel and Restaurant Management Program for the past two years.

Throughout her course work, Donna has truly distinguished herself as an outstanding individual. Academically, I observed her work to be that of a highly motivated, well-organized, conscientious and enthusiastic student. Donna consistently makes a positive contribution to all her classes with her superb grasp of knowledge and keen ability to apply theory.

In addition to her fine intellectual achievements, I also noted her extraordinary leadership within a group/team process, which is one of our departmental emphases. As Event Manager and member of the 1996 and 1997 CCAC Culinary Teams, she consistently demonstrates her technical skills as well as her ability as a motivator of peers, showing sensitivity to the needs of her fellow class members.

Donna has also been selected as my laboratory assistant for the past two years. This is an extremely important departmental position. Among her many responsibilities as laboratory assistant, she assists in all culinary labs, plans and implements all catered events, and maintains the laboratory facility. As lab assistant, Donna also has assumed the responsibilities of our Student Ambassador. In this role, Donna initiates contacts with all new students and thereafter mentors them throughout their academic careers at CCAC.

Therefore, it is without reservation that I recommend Donna Cipriani. Donna has proved to be an invaluable asset to the Hospitality Management Department. She has set her goals high and is determined to succeed. I have the greatest confidence that she will most certainly attain these goals with unqualified success.

Sincerely yours,

Linda Parrish Sullivan

Linda Parrish Sullivan
Professor/Director

McKeesport Hospital

October 21, 1996

1500 Fifth Avenue
McKeesport, PA 15132
Telephone [412] 664-2000

To Whom it May Concern:

The following is an attestation of the work performance of Donna Cipriani.

Miss Cipriani was employed at McKeesport Hospital and worked in the Intensive Care Unit as a nursing assistant under my supervision for several years. During that time she demonstrated knowledge and skills necessary to do her job well. She was a dedicated and hardworking employee. She always displayed a positive attitude and willingness to learn. Miss Cipriani was dependable, accountable and responsible in the performance of her required job duties.

I recommend Miss Cipriani in her endeavors to obtain employment.

Sincerely,

Peggy Hill

Peggy Hill, R.N.
Director of Nursing

**Community College
of Allegheny County**

BOYCE CAMPUS
595 Beatty Road
Monroeville, PA 15146-1395
1 (724) 371-8651

www.ccac.edu

To Whom it May Concern:

I am pleased to write this letter of recommendation for Donna M. Cipriani.

Donna has been the Food Lab Assistant at Boyce Campus since 1996. During that time she worked very closely with the Admissions Office in implementing a recruitment plan for the Hospitality Management program. She developed a database for mailings to local employers. She prepared materials for inclusion in mailings to promote specific courses as well as the Hospitality Management program. She assumed responsibility for the telemarketing component of our prospective student contact program. Donna was in our office every week asking for the updated list of prospects. I never had to chase after Donna; as a matter of fact, I had to work hard to keep up with her level of activity.

Donna attended a recent Monroeville Rotary meeting with me as a student guest. She thoughtfully prepared her presentation and carefully presented her experiences to the group. I was very proud to have her accompany me. She spoke with the various members at our table and mingled before and after the meeting with great confidence.

Donna is a wonderful role model for other students. Her grade point average illustrates her ability in the classroom. She is dedicated to service both at the Campus as well as within the community. Her organizational skills are exceptional as she manages to successfully complete all of her assignments in a timely manner. She is able to work with diverse groups of people to accomplish goals. She is committed to excellence.

I know that Donna has the potential for contributing a great deal to endeavor that she chooses to undertake. Please feel free to contact me if I can provide additional assistance in the review of Donna's credentials.

Sincerely,

Jill Smith

Jill Smith
Director of Public Relations
Community College of Allegheny County

PORTFOLIO TWO

PORTFOLIO OF FRANK CATANZARO, PGA PROFESSIONAL

CONTENTS

- Resume
- Awards and Achievements
- Managing the Golf Shop: Examples

RESUME

FRANK C. CATANZARO

307 Laurie Road
Pittsburgh, PA 15235
(412)724-6771 (work) or 373-1875 (home)
Frankc@Pennnet.net

EDUCATIONAL

B.S., Accounting (1991)
Duquesne University, Pittsburgh, PA

PROFESSIONAL STANDING

PGA Professional

PROFESSIONAL EXPERIENCE

ST. CLAIR COUNTRY CLUB, Upper St. Clair, PA
First Assistant/Teaching Golf Professional (February 1996—Present)
Duties include:

MANAGING GOLF SHOP

- Supervising 38 employees
- Setting up work schedule for golf staff
- Acting for the head Golf Professional in his absence
- Proposing ways of improving shop operation
- Managing the merchandise inventory
- Taking special orders and club repair orders
- Selling merchandise

TEACHING GOLF LESSONS AND CLINICS

- Private lessons for members and community
- Women's clinics
- Junior clinics
- Club fitting
- Tri-State Junior Golf Academy, Seven Springs

(continued)

Continued.

PROFESSIONAL EXPERIENCE (continued)   **Frank C. Catanzaro**

COORDINATING SPECIAL EVENTS/TOURNAMENTS
- Conducting men's and women's events from start to finish
- Duties include: tournament preparation, scheduling golf staff,
- taking scores, and awarding prizes
- Running members' events every Saturday
- Playing with members and guests or in local tournaments

SERVING ON FOLLOWING COMMITTEES
- St. Clair Golf Committee
- St. Clair Greens Committee
- St. Clair Safety Committee

SEWICKLEY HEIGHTS GOLF CLUB, Sewickley, PA
Second Assistant Professional (August 1992–December 1995)

- Managed inventory and club repairs
- Setup special events/tournaments
- Assisted in junior golf clinic
- Played golf with the members

SUN FRESH FOOD SERVICE, INC., Pittsburgh, PA
Sales Representative (January 1992–September 1992)

- Sold services to managers and chefs at restaurants and food stores
- Coordinated warehouse and merchandise

AWARDS AND ACHIEVEMENTS
- Elected to PGA Membership, 1997
- First place, 1997 Club Managers' Tournament
- Low Pro–Fourth place, 1997 Sewickley Heights Pro-Member Stag
- Fourth place 1997, Pro-Assistant
- Completed all two-day events in 1997 and 1996
- First place, 1995 Sewickley Heights Pro-Member Stag (Low pro–Third place)
- Played on Tommy Armour Tour, 1994
- Successfully completed PAT on April 16, 1993 with a score of 149 (Third place)
- Fifth place, 1988 All-State Individual Tournament
- Eighth place, 1987 All-State Individual Tournament
- First place, 1987 Junior College State Team Championship (Captain)
- National Dean's List, 1987–1991
- Student Accounting Association
- Presidential Scholarship
- *Who's Who Among Students in American Colleges,* 1988 and 1989

HOBBIES AND INTERESTS
- Nautilus, free weight, and cardiovascular training
- Playing golf and participating in golf tournaments
- Piano and voice training
- Singing in the church choir

CUSTOM FITTING SYSTEM

CERTIFICATE OF ACHIEVEMENT

This certifies that

Frank Catanzaro

has successfully completed Titleist's Custom Fitting training
and is officially recognized as a

Titleist Custom Fitting Professional

Wally Uihlein

Wally Uihlein, Chairman and CEO
Titleist and Foot-Joy Worldwide

TITLEIST

SERIOUS CLUBS FOR
SERIOUS GOLFERS

Spring 1998

Date

Continued.

THE PROFESSIONAL GOLFERS' ASSOCIATION OF AMERICA

𝕱rank 𝕮. 𝕮atanzaro

Member

Dedicated to the ideal that the name
"PGA Professional" shall be a synonym for honor,
service, fair dealings, personal integrity and fidelity
to the game of golf. It reflects a sense of
responsibility to employers, employees,
manufacturers, amateurs and fellow professionals,
transcending thought of material gain.

Elected June 1997

EXCERPTS:
POLICIES AND PROCEDURES MANUAL

PRO SHOP

St. Clair Country Club
Upper St. Clair, Pennsylvania
Original Copy April 1982, Revised Copy January 1996

ST. CLAIR COUNTRY CLUB
PRO SHOP
Job Description

POSITION TITLE: *First Assistant/Teaching Golf Professional*

Reports to: Head Golf Professional
Supervises: All of the Pro Shop Personnel, through the second assistant Golf Professional and the Caddy Master.

RESPONSIBLE FOR:

- Directing the operation of the Pro Shop.
- Acting for the Head Golf Professional in his or her absence.
- Protecting Club and members' property in the Pro Shop.

SHOP DUTIES:

- Sets up work schedules, reviews them with the Head Professional, puts them in effect, and follows them up.
- Checks staff attendance. Checks that required duties are being performed competently and as scheduled.
- Keeps the Head Professional up to date on activities and problems.
- Proposes ways of improving shop operation.
- Manages the merchandise inventory, proposing purchases to the Head Professional and advising when stock is low.
- Sells merchandise.
- Takes special orders and club repair orders with the Second Assistant Professional.

GOLF DUTIES:

- Runs Saturday events start to finish: signing up members, charging, crediting, and posting results in the locker room.
- Gives golf lessons as events and priority requirements permit.
- Conducts tournaments and special events start to finish.

GENERAL:

- As schedule of other activity permits, the First Assistant may play in local tournaments at St. Clair with members or with own guests, and is entitled to one meal a day in the Grill Room.
- The First Assistant Professional and partner are expected to attend mixed club functions whenever possible, and otherwise fills the position to increase the prestige of St. Clair Country Club and the quality of its service.

ST. CLAIR COUNTRY CLUB
PRO SHOP
Job Description

POSITION TITLE: *Second Assistant Golf Professional*

Reports to: 1st Assistant Golf Professional/Head Golf Professional
Supervises: Pro Shop Staff/Shop Attendants

RESPONSIBILITIES:

- Pro Shop operation
- Supervision of Pro Shop personnel
- Protection of Club equipment and merchandise

PRO SHOP:

- Sees that the shop is opened, kept clean and orderly, and closed on schedule. Arranges attractive displays of merchandise.
- Sets up work schedule for shop attendants and follows up and modifies as required.
- Notifies Head Golf Professional of low stock items.
- Handles special orders. Keeps in touch with vendor and notifies members of receipt of merchandise. Checks receipts of merchandise.
- Writes up purchase orders when none has been issued for goods received.
- Sees that all shop records are kept properly, including daily, weekly, and monthly sales.
- Takes records to the accounting office daily.
- Assists members in signing for carts, greens fees, and caddies.

GOLF:

- Assists in conducting tournaments and special events.
- Works as a Starter on first tee when needed.
- Conducts Wednesday events: As Starter, handling charges and credits, and posting results.
- Assists in Junior Clinic.
- Takes care of golf shop workbench.

GENERAL:

- Plays golf as schedule permits.
- Is entitled to one meal a day in the Grill Room.
- Encourages team operation in all Pro Shop activities.

ST. CLAIR COUNTRY CLUB
PRO SHOP
Job Description

POSITION TITLE: *Shop Attendant*

Reports to: Second Assistant Golf Professional and Head Professional

RESPONSIBLE FOR:

- Assisting in the operation of the Club's Pro Shop.
- Protecting the Pro Shop equipment and merchandise.
- Servicing club members and their guests.

In carrying out these responsibilities, the Attendant performs these and related duties:

OPENING THE SHOP: (see Pro Shop Procedures)

- Checks condition of the shop: clean, orderly, and ready for business.
- Checks merchandise display, especially fast-moving items such as balls and gloves.
- Checks supply of score cards, pencils, and matches.
- Checks messages left on message pad and takes care of applicable items.
- Checks cash drawer, chits, credits, and office supplies.

DAILY ROUTINE:

- Sells merchandise.
- Assists members signing for carts, greens fees, and caddy fees.
- Answers telephone inquiries, puts messages on pad, and makes entries for events and starting times.
- Restocks and rearranges merchandise as needed.
- Receives mail and express packages. These are checked in by the 2nd Assistant Golf Professional.
- Makes out purchase orders for received material as needed.
- Enters postage and express charges in postage book.

CLOSING THE SHOP: (see Pro Shop Procedures)

- Gets records, such as chits, invoices, and P.O.s, ready to go to the accounting office.
- Leaves shop in clean, orderly condition.
- Cooperates with other members of the Pro Shop staff to promote a smooth, efficient operation. Attends to members' and guests' needs to make the Pro Shop an outstanding operation.

GOLF EVENTS: (normally Wednesday, Saturday, and Sunday)

- Assists in recording charges and credits.

ST. CLAIR COUNTRY CLUB
1997
Women's Friday Golf Clinics

PGA PROFESSIONALS

Phil Newcamp, Head Golf Professional; Frank Catanzaro, Assistant Professional
Time: 9:00–11:00 AM (all dates)

Friday, April 18	**IRONS AND CHIPPING**	**Clubs: 5, 6, 7, 8, PW5**

IRONS: The major focus of this lesson will be the full swing for iron play. Areas of discussion will include proper positions throughout the swing and the importance of the proper grip, setup, and stance in permitting a good swing to occur.

CHIPPING: This session is dedicated to the most neglected aspect of the game. Learn the proper technique and turn three shots into two.

IRONS: 9:00–10:00 AM

CHIPPING: 10:00–11:00 AM

Friday, April 25	**WOODS & PITCHING**	**Clubs: Woods, PW, SW**

WOODS: Building upon the principles of the full swing, we will concentrate on tee shots and fairway woods.

PITCHING: As with chipping this area of the game is often neglected. Learn the proper technique and club selection to lower your score.

PITCHING: 9:00–10:00 AM

WOODS: 10:00–11:00 AM

Friday, May 2	**PUTTING & BUNKER SHOTS**	**Clubs: Putter, SW**

PUTTING: The major focus of this lesson will be the proper mechanics of putting. Other topics covered will include reading greens, proper etiquette while on the green, and the rules of golf that pertain to the putting surface.

BUNKER SHOTS: The most troublesome shot in golf will become the easiest. A good sand wedge, the right technique, and practice is all you need!

PUTTING: 9:00–10:00 AM

SAND PLAY: 10:00–11:00 AM

Continued. **EXAMPLES**

WOMEN'S GOLF CLINIC TIPS

GRIP: Left Hand–Club should lie diagonally from the first joint of the little finger to the last joint of the index finger.

Right Hand–Overlap little finger of right hand over index finger of left hand. The rest of the right hand should be gripped in the fingertips covering the left thumb. The right thumb is on the left side of the shaft.

The "V" formed by the thumb and the index finger on both hands should point towards your right shoulder.

Remember to grip the club in a way that gives you control over it, but not so tight that you restrict the freedom of motion in your arms. Compare this to holding a pen in order to sign your name. If you grip the pen too tightly, you will not be able to freely write your name. If your grip on the pen is too loose, you will not have enough control over the pen to sign your name. It will fall out of your hand.

STANCE: The stance is taken with the feet approximately shoulder width apart. The stance will be slightly wider for longer shots and increasingly narrow as the shots to the target become shorter. The ball is positioned slightly left of center for a right-handed player. As the shots become shorter in length, the ball moves toward the middle of the stance. The knees are flexed and the body is free of tension.

BACKSWING: The backswing is an important part of the golf swing. It is used in order to develop consistency, timing, and rhythm. Certain positions within the backswing help to determine the success of the shot.

The arms should swing freely up and around the body as the weight shifts to the right side. The change of direction from the backswing to the forward swing is a free, smooth transition.

FOLLOW-THROUGH: Always work to achieve a good finish position, regardless of the quality of the shot. Finish with your hands and arms up and over the forward shoulder. Your weight has shifted to your left side and your [belt buckle] now faces the target.

DRILLS

FEET TOGETHER DRILL:

1. Tee the ball up slightly.
2. Use a seven iron.
3. Place your feet very close together so that your body's lateral movement is greatly reduced.
4. Strike several balls without any concern for distance.
5. Maintain your balance and swing your arms up and around your body.

TOE UP DRILL:

1. Tee the ball up slightly.
2. Take a stance that is slightly narrower than normal.
3. Take the clubhead back by swinging the arms freely to waist height (the toe of the club should be pointing skyward at this point).
4. Swing through the ball, making sure the toe of the club faces skyward at waist height on the follow-through.

KEY TO DRILLS:

Golf is played along parallel lines. Your feet, knees, hips, and shoulders should all be parallel to your target line at address. Consequently, when you swing the club, the shaft should also be parallel to the target line at the following four positions:

1. waist high during the backswing
2. at the top or completion of your backswing
3. at waist height during the follow-through
4. at the completion of the follow-through

PUTTING

GRIP: Choose a grip that feels comfortable to you. Many different styles of putting will produce good results if a few basic fundamentals are followed. Concerning the grip, the hands must be able to work together and the grip pressure must be light.

STANCE: As with the full swing, in putting you need to be parallel to the target line in order to have success. This is especially true of the forearms, shoulders, and eyes. Your eyes should be directly over the ball and parallel to your target line. The ball should be positioned opposite the inside edge of your left foot (for a right-handed putter).

STROKE: Take the putter back only as far as is necessary to allow the ball to go firmly in the hole. The Putter Must Accelerate Through The Ball! Use your right foot as a guide for the length of the backstroke, and then follow through the same distance. Keep the putter blade low to the ground, with a smooth, firm stroke.

PUTTING DRILLS

1. Make ten putts in a row from three feet away. Pick a straight putt when doing this drill. How about 25 in a row?
2. Place 12 balls around a hole, each about four feet away. Pick a hole that is positioned on a slope for this drill. Work your way around the circle and putt each ball toward the hole. If you happen to miss, just go to the next ball.
3. Take three balls and putt the first one to a distance of about 20 feet. Without looking up to see where the first putt stopped, take the next ball and putt it three feet past the first one. Again, do not look up. Now take the third ball and putt it three feet short of the first ball. Now you may look to see how you have done. Vary the distances and do this again.
4. Place a straight line of balls (4–6) approximately 10 inches apart, leading away from the hole. Start with the ball nearest the hole and try to make all the putts.

CHIPPING

GRIP: Use the standard grip that you use on full swings. Choke down on the club almost to the end of the grip. The club will feel lighter and you will have more control. Grip the club just tightly enough to control it. Position the hands slightly ahead of the ball (towards the hole).

STANCE: Align the club face directly at the target. Keep the grooves on the clubface perpendicular to the target line. Your feet should be aimed slightly to the right of the target line. Your stance should be narrow, with a majority of the weight placed on your left foot. Place the ball in the center of your stance.

STROKE: Allow wrists to break slightly on the backswing. Take the club back only as far as you will need in order to have the ball reach the hole. You Must Accelerate Through The Ball! Hit the ball on the downswing, striking the ball, then the turf. This will occur naturally. Allow the weight of the clubhead to propel the ball. Listen for the proper sound. The follow-through is only as long as the backstroke. Finish with your left wrist firm and the back of the left hand facing the target.

DRILL: Using a seven or eight iron, PRACTICE, PRACTICE, PRACTICE.

PITCHING: GRIP and STANCE–Same as chipping. Use Pitching Wedge or Sand Wedge.

SWING: Take a backswing to approximately waist height. Allow the wrists to break naturally. Allow the clubface to open as you swing back so that the toe of the club points to the sky at waist height. With a smooth transition from the backswing to the downstroke, allow the weight of the clubhead to lift the ball into the air. Never physically try to lift the ball. The right shoulder will swing under your chin as you follow through to about the same height as on your backswing.

DRILLS AND THOUGHTS

Pitch golf balls over an object such as your golf bag. You will find that the ball will go up only when you swing down and through the ball. If these shots are rolling along the ground and not getting airborne, you are probably trying to lift the shot.

A good habit on the full swing is to always finish in good balance with the weight transferred to your forward foot and your [belt buckle] facing the target. Even when the shot is not as good as you would like, finish the swing in good position. This will help you to expect a good shot because you made a good swing.

Swing the clubhead with a body that is virtually free of tension. Allow the club to swing and come into contact with the ball only because the ball happens to be in the way of the clubhead. Remember, you can make a great swing and miss the ball if it was not positioned in the path of your swing.

Above all, remember that golf is a game. Make it a fun game by having CONFIDENCE in the desired results of you swing. The best players in the world miss hit shots every day.

EXAMPLES Continued.

JUNIOR GOLF CAMP

WEDNESDAY, JUNE 17, 1997	
Clubs Needed:	5 or 7 Iron and Putter
8:30–8:45	Orientation, Rules, Safety
8:45–9:15	Grip, Aim Setup, Overall Swing Motion
9:15–10:30	Ball Striking, Putting
10:30–11:00	Putting Contest–Prized Awarded

THURSDAY, JUNE 18, 1997		
Clubs Needed:	Wood, 5, 7, 9 Irons and Pitching Wedge	
8:30–8:45	Rules, Safety	
8:45–9:30	Group 1–Chipping & Pitching	Group 2–Full Shots
9:30–10:15	Group 1–Full Shots	Group 2–Chipping & Pitching
10:15–11:00	Chipping Contest–Prized Awarded	

FRIDAY, JUNE 19, 1997	
Clubs Needed:	All
8:30–9:00	Rules, Etiquette
9:00–11:00	"Scramble" Team Competition–Prized Awarded

Junior Members

All Players Must Register In The Pro Shop Before Teeing Off.

Certified Junior Members and guests 12 years of age or older are the only children permitted on the Golf Courses (18 Hole & Terrace Nine).

A Junior Member shall be the son or daughter of a Voting member, a Senior member (or a deceased Voting or Senior member), at least twelve years of age, who has not attained his or her 24th birthday. The professional golf staff conducts an annual Junior Golf Clinic. The successful completion of the clinic leads to the classification of Certified Junior Member. This certification may also be secured through the professional golf staff by demonstration of proficiency at the game and knowledge of the rules of golf.

Qualified Junior Members may play on Terrace Nine at any time on Mondays, providing there are no other scheduled events. Juniors may play any time on Tuesdays and after 2:00 p.m. on Thursdays. An unaccompanied Junior Member may tee off by 10:00 a.m. on Friday morning, or after 10:00 a.m. with a parent or active member, and after 2:30 p.m. on Saturdays and Sundays. A Certified Junior Member may start after 1:00 p.m. on Saturdays and Sundays if playing with a parent. A Certified Male Junior Member age 14 or older may play with his father on Sunday mornings and must use a caddy or cart. A Junior Member May Not Bring A Guest.

Sons and daughters of Social Members are not considered Junior Golf Members, but, for a fee, may participate in Junior Golf Programs on Monday mornings.

A male must be 21 years of age to use the Men's Locker Room and the 19th Hole.

SAFETY FIRST

Stop and Look Before You Swing—Always make sure that no one is near you when you swing, both in practice and in play. Also make sure that no one is ahead of you where your shot might hit someone. When you are playing any shot, remember this rule: Stop and Look Before You Swing! When others are playing, stand quietly in a safe position. One recommended position to be used whenever possible is to face the golfer who is playing, standing at least three full paces, or ten feet away. This position is normally where a caddie stands.

If your shot goes off in a direction in which it could hit someone, shout "Fore!" Shouting "Fore," however, is no substitute for safe thinking before taking your shot.

Golf Courtesy or Etiquette—The first section of the Official United States Golf Association Rules of Golf discusses golf courtesy, or good manners on the golf course. Striving to be a good golfer is important, but golf courtesy is equally important and will make you many friends who will enjoy playing with you.

Consider Others—Treat your fellow golfers as you would like to be treated. This is a good rule for life, both on and off the golf course. On the course, being quiet and not moving around while others are playing will make the game more enjoyable for everyone.

Take Care of the Course—Always remember to help take good care of the playing areas while you play. Replace divots or chunks of grass. These divots will grow back if replaced right away, but the grass will die if it is left out of the ground. When you have played out of a bunker, rake the sand smooth before leaving it. Repair any ball marks caused by your ball landing on the green.

PLAYING THE GAME

How the Game of Golf Is Played—The idea of the game of golf is to move the ball from a starting place (the tee), swinging as many times as it may take until you get it to the green and into the finish place (the hole, or cup). The object of the game is to do this in as few strokes as possible. You count every swing, including penalty strokes and whiffs (misses) at the ball, but not practice swings away from the ball. Your score for the hole is the total number of strokes you took from the tee to the hole, or cup, in the green.

Scoring—Each hole will have a number or score listed for it, which is called par. This is the standard of excellence that golfers shoot for when they begin the hole. Your scores will be much higher than par when you first begin to play golf, and your scores will go down as you practice and improve your skills. Depending on the length of the hole, a hole may be rated for a 3-stroke, 4-stroke, or 5-stroke par. Although you may not be shooting for a par, you can use the par standard to help measure your own skill on different holes.

Golfers who shoot close to par use special terms for their scores on a hole. Finishing the hole with the same score as par is called making par. Scoring one stroke under par is a birdie, and two strokes under par is an eagle, Scoring one stroke over par is a bogey, and two strokes over par is a double bogey.

Continued.

THE SCORE CARD

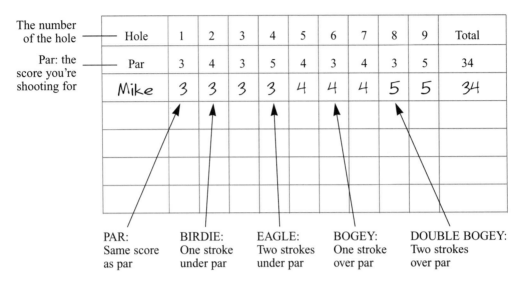

The number of the hole ——— Hole

Par: the score you're shooting for ——— Par

Hole	1	2	3	4	5	6	7	8	9	Total
Par	3	4	3	5	4	3	4	3	5	34
Mike	3	3	3	3	4	4	4	5	5	34

PAR: Same score as par

BIRDIE: One stroke under par

EAGLE: Two strokes under par

BOGEY: One stroke over par

DOUBLE BOGEY: Two strokes over par

A FINAL SWING CHECKLIST

Here is a routine to line up and play a shot:

1. Stand behind the ball and look at the target line to the target.
2. Take your stance, aiming the club and the body parallel toward the target.
3. Look at the target. Imagine a good shot.
4. Make a smooth, one-two rhythm swing.

St. Clair Country Club   DATE: _____

| FORWARD TEES | JUNIOR PAR | | | | HANDICAP STROKES | | | | HOLE | | | +
− |
| | BOYS | | GIRLS | | | | | | | | | |
	BEGINNER	INTERMEDIATE	BEGINNER	INTERMEDIATE								
296	6	5	7	5	8				1			
147	4	3	4	3	9				2			
462	8	6	9	7	1				3			
406	7	6	8	6	2				4			
319	6	5	7	5	7				5			
224	5	4	6	4	5				6			
305	6	5	7	5	4				7			
216	5	4	5	4	3				8			
287	6	5	7	5	6				9			
2662	53	43	60	44					TOTAL			

Scorer _____   Attest _____

Always wait to play until the group ahead is off the green.

SEQUENCE OF ORDER OF PLAY

Always be ready to play when it's your turn.

Maintain a Steady Pace—Play each hole without delay. Be ready to play when it is your turn to hit. Those farthest from the green or cup usually hit first. Limit yourself to no more than one full practice swing before each shot.

Don't tee off until the group in the fairway is out of your driving distance.

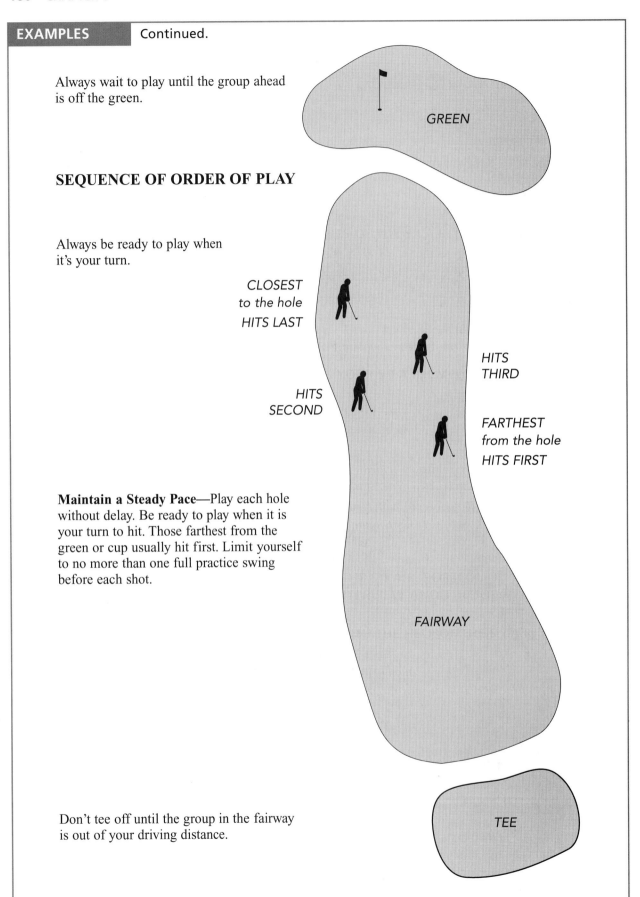

GREEN

CLOSEST to the hole HITS LAST

HITS THIRD

HITS SECOND

FARTHEST from the hole HITS FIRST

FAIRWAY

TEE

COORDINATING SPECIAL EVENTS AND TOURNAMENTS

1997 WOMEN'S GOLF ASSOCIATION EVENTS AND DATES

Date/Day	Event
April 3, Thurs.	Opening Breakfast—*8:45 a.m.*
April 10, Thurs.	Event Day
April 17, Thurs.	Ace Day
May 15, Thurs.	Ace Day
May 22, Thurs.	Florida Scrambles
May 25, Sun.	Memorial Day Mixed Event—*1:30 p.m. Shotgun*
May 29, Thurs.	Massey Cup
June 5, Thurs.	Spring Invitation—*8:30 a.m. Shotgun*
June 6, Fri.	Interclub (at St. Clair)
June 12, Thurs.	Flag Day
June 17, Tues.	Trotter Cup
June 19, Thurs.	Trotter Cup
June 22, Sun.	Mixed Event—*1:30 p.m. Shotgun*
June 26, Thurs.	Member-Member—*8:00 a.m. Shotgun*
July 3, Thurs.	Red, White & Blue Tournament
July 6, Sun.	Independence Day Mixed Event—*1:30 p.m. Shotgun*
July 10, Thurs.	Seniors' Tournament
July 11, Fri.	Interclub (at Chartiers)
July 17, Thurs.	Queen Bee—Ace Day
July 24, Thurs.	Queen Bee
July 29, Tues.	Queen Bee—Rain Date
July 31, Thurs.	Grandmothers' Tournament
Aug. 1, Fri.	Interclub (at South Hills)
Aug. 2, Sat.	Mixed Invitation—*1:30 p.m. Shotgun*
Aug. 7, Thurs.	Club Championship First Round
Aug. 8, Fri.	Club Championship Second Round
Aug. 14, Thurs.	Club Championship Third Round
Aug. 21, Thurs.	Club Championship Rain Date—Ace Day
Aug. 28, Thurs.	Fall Invitation—*8:30 a.m. Shotgun*
Aug. 31, Sun.	Labor Day Mixed Event—*1:30 p.m. Shotgun*
Sept. 4, Thurs.	Mulligan Day
Sept. 11, Thurs.	Derby Day—*8:00 a.m. Shotgun*
Sept. 14, Sun.	Mixed Championship—*1:30 p.m. Shotgun*
Sept. 18, Thurs.	Three Queens and a King—*8:00 a.m. Shotgun*—Ace Day
Sept. 25, Thurs.	Ace Tournament—Final Day of Competition
Oct. 2, Thurs.	Closing Event and Brunch

1997 WOMEN'S GOLF ASSOCIATION 9-HOLERS' EVENTS AND DATES

Date/Day	Event
April 3, Thurs.	Opening Breakfast—*8:45 a.m.*
April 10, Thurs.	Event Day
April 17, Thurs.	Event Day
April 24, Thurs.	Event Day
May 1, Thurs.	Event Day
May 8, Thurs.	Event Day
May 15, Thurs.	Gracie Weiss Event
May 22, Thurs.	Florida Scrambles
May 25, Sun.	Memorial Day Mixed Event—*1:30 p.m. Shotgun*
May 29, Thurs.	Event Day
June 5, Thurs.	Grandmothers' Tournament
June 8, Sun.	Couples' Twilight Event—*5:00 p.m.*
June 12, Thurs.	Event Day
June 19, Thurs.	Invitation
June 22, Sun.	Mixed Event—*1:30 p.m. Shotgun*
June 26, Thurs.	Event Day
July 3, Thurs.	Event Day
July 6, Sun.	Independence Day Mixed Event—*1:30 p.m. Shotgun*
July 10, Thurs.	Queen Bee—First Round
July 13, Sun.	Couples' Twilight Event—*5:00 p.m.*
July 17, Thurs.	Queen Bee—Second Round
July 24, Thurs.	Queen Bee—Rain Date
July 31, Thurs.	Event Day
Aug. 2, Sat.	Mixed Invitation—*1:30 p.m. Shotgun*
Aug. 7, Thurs.	Club Championship—First Round
Aug. 8, Fri.	Couples' Twilight Event—*5:00 p.m.*
Aug. 12, Tues.	Club Championship—Second Round
Aug. 14, Thurs.	Club Championship—Third Round
Aug. 21, Thurs.	Club Championship—Rain Date
Aug. 28, Thurs.	Guest Day
Aug. 31, Sun.	Labor Day Mixed Event—*1:30 p.m. Shotgun*
Sept. 4, Thurs.	Derby Day
Sept. 11, Thurs.	Event Day
Sept. 12, Fri.	Couples' Twilight Event—*4:00 p.m.*
Sept. 14, Sun.	Mixed Championship—*1:30 p.m. Shotgun*
Sept. 18, Thurs.	Event Day
Sept. 25, Thurs.	Event Day
Oct. 2, Thurs.	Closing Event and Brunch

Continued.

ST. CLAIR COUNTRY CLUB

TOURNAMENT PREPARATIONS

Event: _____   # of Entries _____

Date: _____   Entry Fee: _____

Starting Times: _____

Format: _____

JOB	STAFF MEMBER RESPONSIBLE	COMPLETE BY	SPECIAL INSTRUCTIONS
Pairings			
Cart Tags			
Scorecards			
Scoreboard			
Rule Sheet			
Pin Sheet			
Driving Range Setup			
Bag Room Staff			
Caddies			
Billing			
Tee Sheet Preparation			
Grounds Special Instructions			
Contests			
Ranger			

ST. CLAIR COUNTRY CLUB

TOURNAMENT SUMMARY

Event: _____

Dates: _____

Format: _____

_____

Number of Players: _____

List of Winners: _____

_____

_____

_____

_____

_____

Special Event Winners: _____

_____

Highlights: _____

Problems: _____

_____

_____

Changes for Next Year: _____

_____

_____

_____

_____

_____

Attach a list of participants to this form

PORTFOLIO OF CONSTRUCTION & HISTORICAL RESTORATION PROJECTS

RESUME

KEITH EUSTACE

RD 51, Box 456A, Ligonier, PA   15658   (412) 325-6777

OBJECTIVE: CONSTRUCTION MANAGEMENT/FACILITIES MANAGEMENT

To expedite and oversee efficient operation of projects, personnel, and resources by contributing proven ability to:

- Identify client needs and project requirements
- Facilitate profitable and timely completion of projects
- Supervise contractors and employees
- Communicate confidently and productively with clients, associates, and employees

QUALIFICATIONS: A highly successful building construction manager and designer with outstanding experience and expertise in:

- Organizing/Prioritizing
- Planning/Implementing
- Problem Solving/Resolving
- Managing/Directing
- Supervising/Leading

- Motivating/Empowering
- Marketing/Targeting
- Liaison/Negotiating
- Customer Relations/Service

ACHIEVEMENTS:

- Acquired new clients and initiated new projects with existing clients, broadening organization's business base and playing a major role in doubling company turnover.
- Supervised projects and personnel to maximize profits, improve quality of work, and enhance completion within established time frame.
- Increased company's profitability by $30,000 through the assumption of additional responsibilities.
- Built trusting and lasting relationships with clients, agents, and employees, resulting in mutual satisfaction and repeat business.
- Created and implemented original design and technical solutions saving $15,000 and reducing completion time by one month.
- Motivated reluctant employees to comply with and follow safety regulations, avoiding injury and litigation.
- Demonstrated ability to quickly resolve problems, leading to efficient project completion and client satisfaction.

(continued)

KEITH EUSTACE

page 2

PROFESSIONAL EXPERIENCE:

Outstanding comprehensive management experience in building construction and historic rehabilitation. Superior knowledge of the industry as a result of performing the duties of **Tradesperson, Designer, Safety Officer, Historic Preservation Officer, Code Enforcer, Construction Manager, Marketer** and **Contract Negotiator.**

ADDITIONAL TRAINING:

National Joint Industries Training Board Carpentry Certification, National Building Industries Building Construction Certification, National Federation of Builders Building Materials Certification, Construction Industry Training Board Certification in Construction Safety, Site Plant, and Equipment. Specialized training in Building Code Regulations, Lime Applications, and Insulation and Ventilation.

EXPANDED PROFESSIONAL EXPERIENCE

SENIOR CONSTRUCTION MANAGER 1969–1997
Boshers (Cholsey) Ltd., Cholsey, Oxfordshire, England

Clients: Dealt directly with the client from the initial inquiry/lead to the tender stage and throughout the course of the contract and the Defects Liability Period. Handled any further work/contracts for the same client.

Architects: Conducted the initial meetings; liaised with the estimators on tender negotiations; handled contract preliminaries; conducted site meetings; recorded variations; liaised on preparation of final accounts.

Local Authorities: Dealt with aspects of Planning Permission. Listed Building Consents and Building Regulations.

Contracts: Liaised between clients and architects; set up contract works; handled programming and progress chasing; scheduled materials and subcontractors; handled coordination of information, site administration, technical input; recorded variations; completion of contract; and agreeing and actioning correction of defects.

Sites: Managed site agents; identified site labor requirements and organized accordingly; selected and managed subcontractors; handled cost control, coordination of public utilities, site welfare, and site safety, including safety training, and preparation of risk assessments and work method statements.

Miscellaneous: Prepared, where required, drawings for whole schemes, parts of schemes, or details, including joinery.

PORTFOLIO CONTENTS FOR KEITH EUSTACE

PROJECTS	AWARDS
1. Hillfields Farm, Lower Basildon, Berkshire	
2. Basildon Park, Basildon, Berkshire	
3. Historic Farm Buildings, Sunningwell, Oxfordshire	Certificate of Recommendation of the Royal Institute of British Architects
4. West Ilsey Training Stable, West Ilsey, Berkshire	
5. Wormsley Park, Stokenchurch, Buckinghamshire	The Malcolm Dean Award by Wycombe District Council
6. Winterbook House, Wallingford, Oxfordshire	
7. Raglan Court, Goldsmiths Land, Wallingford, Oxfordshire	Award from Royal Institute of British Architects
8. The Barley Mow Public House, Building Clifton Hampden, Oxfordshire	Award from the local Historical Society

PROPERTY	**Hillfields Farm, Lower Basildon, Berkshire**
CLIENT	**Intereal Estates**
CONTRACT	Erection of High Quality Building to House Client's Collection of Classic Motor Cars

- A basically circular building with a steel frame, clad with handmade bricks, and a traditional wooden roof system clad with handmade clay tiles.
- Incorporated into the design of the building were early Victorian stained glass and crystal glass panels. A crystal dome light was also used as a lighting centerpiece.
- The car collection included many classic British and European cars such as M.G.s, Jaguars, Rolls Royces, Mercedes, and also a very early Cadillac with wooden-framed and -spoked wheels.

CONSTRUCTIONAL CHALLENGES

- Setting out the circular building with its rectangular additions at each end.
- Cutting of semicircular roof plates.
- Junction of rectangular sections of roof to conical sections.
- Cutting and fixing of ceiling panels in 10' x 4' sections to underside of rafters.
- Laying and leveling of anhydrous screed in one operation over underfloor heating system. (This prevents curling of screed at bay joints.)
- Design and making of large curbed hardwood doors.
- Maintaining high standard of finish to ceiling panel joints and painted finish to internal fair-faced brick walls.
- Painting of floor with specially mixed epoxy resin quick-drying floor finish.

PROPERTY   **Basildon Park, Basildon, Berkshire**
A Palladian Mansion Designed by John Carr of York

CLIENT   **The National Trust**

CONTRACT   Provision of Public Access Facilities to Grade I Listed Building and
Restoration of Deteriorated Facade

- Once the family home of Lord Iliffe, passed to the National Trust.
- Provision to be made for public access, car parking, ticketing, and public restroom facilities.
- Installation of commercial catering facilities in vaulted basement.
- Inconspicuous strengthening of delicate cantilevered carved stone staircase.
- Reinforcement of very ornate plaster moulded ceilings.
- Cutting of new access openings in 3'0"-thick stone-faced brick walls.
- Provision and installation of period showcases for collections of shells, *objects d'art,* and costumes.
- Restoration of stone pediment and coping to the North Lodge, including new 7 lb. cast lead coping.

CONSTRUCTIONAL
CHALLENGES

- To carry out all structural works without causing damage to surrounding detailed and fragile plaster and timber ornamentation and rare silk wall hangings.

- Cutting openings through stone-cased walls with sometimes insecure cores without causing settlement of the surrounding structure.

- Steel reinforcing of stone staircase with minimal disruption, and making good to existing wall and soffit finishes.

- Careful and vibration-free removal of two layers of steel-tongued timber floorboards to gain access to ornamental plastered ceiling framework. Very careful insertion of steel reinforcement and plating to ceiling framework and refixing of floor boarding.

- Carrying out work whilst National Trust staff prepared displays and had scheduled "open days."

- Completing work on schedule despite many changes and unforeseen works to meet official Grand Opening date.

Continued. **EXAMPLES**

PROPERTY **Historic Farm Buildings, Sunningwell, Oxfordshire**

CLIENT **The Pilkington Trust**

CONTRACT Pioneering Conversion of Listed Farm Facility

- Conversion of 5 no. historic oak-framed, brick, flint and stone-clad farm barns and associated surroundings into 6 dwellings.
- Special attention had to be paid to maintain rural appearance of development as a whole unit and to utilize as much of existing structure as possible.

CONSTRUCTIONAL CHALLENGES
- Lowering first floor levels, in some cases as much as 4 feet, to provide adequate headroom with associated support and underpinning of existing brick and flint walls.
- Tanking of lowered floors to prevent water penetration.
- Support and repair to oak barn timbers during construction.
- Insertion of new door and window openings without jeopardizing structural integrity of timber structure.

OTHER *Awarded Certificate of Recommendation of the Royal Institute of British Architects.*

PROPERTY **West Ilsey Training Stables, West Ilsey, Berkshire**

CLIENT **H.R.H., The Queen**

CONTRACT Construction of Stable Block and Loose Boxes at Training Establishment Owned by Her Majesty.

CONSTRUCTIONAL CHALLENGES
- Making sure everything ran like clockwork!

EXAMPLES	Continued.

PROPERTY **Wormsley Park, Stokenchurch, Buckinghamshire**

CLIENT **John Paul Getty, Jr.**

CONTRACT Refurbishment of Many Buildings on 20,000 Acre Estate, including:

- Main house,
- Fitting out of library for collection of rare books,
- Refurbishment of the Home Farm,
- Construction of traditional English cricket pavilion with thatched roof and cricket bat balustrade overlooking client's private cricket ground,
- Construction of thatched mobile cricket scoreboard,
- Construction of walled garden and associated horticultural buildings.

CONSTRUCTIONAL
CHALLENGES
- Maintaining good relationship with the client's many representatives.
- Ensuring absolute quality of labor and materials at all times.
- Completing work within very tight time frames.

OTHER *Awarded the Malcolm Dean Award by Wycombe District Council.*

Continued.

PROPERTY   **Winterbrook House, Wallingford, Oxfordshire**

CLIENT   **Lady Mallowan**—better known as Agatha Christie, the well-known mystery writer

CONTRACT   Regular Maintenance, Remodeling, and Redecoration of Victorian Listed Building, Outbuildings, and Grounds

- Regular maintenance of the Listed building and grounds together with a private squash court building in the grounds.

- Lady Mallowan was an elderly lady when I worked for her, looking nothing like the photograph which always appeared on the rear cover of her books. The house was full of mementos as a result of her success as a writer. One, in particular, was a small reproduction of a handgun, mounted on a plaque and awarded by *Ellery Queen's Mystery Magazine.*

  When she died, she was buried in the local Cholsey Church cemetery, which is now a *must* for all Agatha Christie buffs.

EXAMPLES	Continued.

PROPERTY **Raglan Court, Goldsmiths Lane, Wallingford, Oxfordshire**

CLIENT **Raglan Housing Association**

CONTRACT Demolition of Existing Industrial Property, Erection of New Buildings in Traditional Materials to Provide Housing and Assisted Living Facility.

CONSTRUCTIONAL CHALLENGES

- Very restricted access to site, which bordered a vital thoroughfare road. Materials, not able to be stacked on site, had to be brought in daily and unloaded before traffic started.
- Contaminated soil from old foundry processes had to be safely removed and disposed of.
- Site was on made-up ground with medieval plague pits, previous industrial pits, etc., necessitating silent piling and excavations up to 22 feet deep. High water table and unstable ground required de-watering system for traditional foundations and sewage installations.
- Building bordering road was crescent shaped with associated setting out problems with roof/purling details and roof slating.
- Obtaining and fixing genuine Welsh handmade slates from quarry with limited production.

OTHER *Winner of Award from Royal Institute of British Architects.*

Continued.

PROPERTY   **The Barley Mow Public House, Clifton Hampden, Oxfordshire**

CLIENT   **Chef and Brewer Inns**

CONTRACT   Complete Refurbishment of 14th-Century Inn Following Major Fire.

- This famous old building, which is mentioned in the well-known Jerome K. Jerome book, *Three Men in a Boat,* was seriously damaged as a result of a fire started by an electrical fault.

- The Inn is one of the earliest surviving examples of a cruck-framed building and still retains the original oak crucks, some purlins, rafters and floor joists. The fire consumed some of the original timbers, but fortunately was mainly confined to the roof area, including the thatch.

- Unfortunately, the damage done by the fire hoses saturating the old structure was as severe as the fire itself. The original "wattle and daub" wall panels suffered particularly from water damage and had to be restored.

- The Inn was completely restored including new thatch, replacing burnt timbers and remaking the "wattle and daub" panels in the traditional way, that is, with hazel wattle and lime mortar daubing.

EXAMPLES Continued.

CONSTRUCTIONAL
CHALLENGES

- Drying out the building in the most economical way without drying it too fast and thus causing more damage to the original framing and finishes.

- Careful piecing in of new oak members to the original, using traditional methods such as scarfing with oak dowels.

- Remaking the original "wattle and daub" panels in the original fashion with no nails and no cement.

- Stripping back the decorated surfaces to allow the lime plaster and oak paneling to dry out and then, once dry, replicating the finishes with traditional materials such as lime wash on walls and wax-based polishes on exposed timbers.

- Re-thatching the building with the embellished ridge and dormer window details. The new thatch was treated before laying with a fire retardant solution.

- Despite the high standard of care and attention to detail, the Inn had to be open in time for the lucrative summer tourist trade.

OTHER

Award from the local Historical Building Society.

Index